SUCCEEDING

at

SUCCESSION

How Family Businesses *Can Share* Power, Money, *and* Control
...*and Still* Remain a Family

SUCCEEDING

at

SUCCESSION

TAMAR MILO, Ph.D.

Copyright © 2018 by Tamar Milo.

All rights reserved. No part of this book may be used or reproduced in any manner whatsoever without prior written consent of the author, except as provided by the United States of America copyright law.

Published by Advantage, Charleston, South Carolina.
Member of Advantage Media Group.

ADVANTAGE is a registered trademark, and the Advantage colophon is a trademark of Advantage Media Group, Inc.

Printed in the United States of America.

10 9 8 7 6 5 4 3 2 1

ISBN: 978-1-64225-058-9
LCCN: 2018953902

Cover design by Melanie Cloth.
Layout design by Mary Hamilton.
Painting on cover by Valerio Berruti, *Family Values* (2002)

This publication is designed to provide accurate and authoritative information in regard to the subject matter covered. It is sold with the understanding that the publisher is not engaged in rendering legal, accounting, or other professional services. If legal advice or other expert assistance is required, the services of a competent professional person should be sought.

Advantage Media Group is proud to be a part of the Tree Neutral® program. Tree Neutral offsets the number of trees consumed in the production and printing of this book by taking proactive steps such as planting trees in direct proportion to the number of trees used to print books. To learn more about Tree Neutral, please visit **www.treeneutral.com**.

Advantage Media Group is a publisher of business, self-improvement, and professional development books and online learning. We help entrepreneurs, business leaders, and professionals share their Stories, Passion, and Knowledge to help others Learn & Grow. Do you have a manuscript or book idea that you would like us to consider for publishing? Please visit **advantagefamily.com** or call **1.866.775.1696**.

This book is dedicated to Hillel, whose love and support empower my journey. To my loved children, Matan, Sage and Donna, who taught me the most valuable lessons. To my grandchildren, Uri and Naomi, the joy of my life.

TABLE OF CONTENTS

PREFACE — xi

ACKNOWLEDGEMENTS — xiii

CHAPTER 1 — 1
Breaking the Silence

CHAPTER 2 — 15
My Experience Being in a Family Business

CHAPTER 3 — 27
Why Your Family Must Dare to Ask the *Why* Questions

CHAPTER 4 — 43
Making the Younger Generation the Catalyst for Change

CHAPTER 5 — 57
It's All about Ownership

CHAPTER 6 — 73
The Unspoken Evils of Wealth

CHAPTER 7 — 91
What Do Parents Really Owe Their Children?

CHAPTER 8 — 109
Work with Your Natural Partners

CHAPTER 9 — 125
Create Tangible Results

CHAPTER 10 — 145
Family Agreements

CHAPTER 11 — 169
How Is It Done?

CHAPTER 12 — 189
Should We Talk?

PREFACE

My understanding of the complex systems called Family Businesses has evolved over time. At first I could see only the differences among families, but gradually I started to see some commonalities, until finally I came to the realization that the dilemmas specific to family businesses are universal. The solutions, however, have to be tailored to each family and to each situation. This book addresses these universal dilemmas, and tells the stories of many families that dealt with these issues, each in their own way.

My country is characterized by a relatively young economy that is based on an ancient culture. Each chapter of this book opens with a quote from the old wisdom of Jewish texts. The relevance of these texts to our reality is eye-opening. The stories and tools I offer as solutions are based on the reality of our young economy—transitions from founders to second generations, from second to third, and in rare cases even from third to fourth generations.

I am a great believer in the power of successors! Throughout the book I show time and again how a successor can affect the destiny of a family and of the family business, even before they receive their official mandate and authority. With this power comes great responsibility, and this book attempts to empower successors to succeed on their challenging journeys.

It is my hope that those who read this book will take from it the feeling that "Yes, we can"—that it is possible to succeed, and they are not alone in this endeavor.

ACKNOWLEDGEMENTS

I have wanted to write this book for years. This wish, or maybe dream, was finally fulfilled due to the love and support of my partner to life, Hillel. Thank you for believing in me, and for dreaming the book, even before I dared doing so.

Judy Stern Peck, whom I met many years ago through her excellent book "Money and Meaning", and who later became my colleague on a consulting project, was the mid-wife nurse, for the birth of this book. Thank you Judy for making it happen.

Special thanks go to my two colleagues, Menahem Yablonski and Tal Yahav. In the many years we worked together, each of them brought significant added value, and contributed insights, that enriched my understanding of families in business, their needs and their dynamics. Thank you Menahem and Tal for the teamwork, and for your valuable contributions to this book.

The ancient wisdom that can be found in the Jewish texts has been part of my life since I remember myself. I wanted to bring some of it into this book, in the way of quotes that would open each chapter, adding the time perspective to current issues. It would not have happened without my teacher, Mordechai Bar-Or, who suggested appropriate texts, and brought to me some, which were previously unknown to me.

My family members, Hillel and Sage Milo, together with my friend Daniel Goldman, were the readers of each chapter of the book. Their comments and suggestions provided value to the content and reassurance to me in my work. Thanks to all of you for your valuable assistance.

Geneva Burleigh made the magic transformation of my ideas, into a cohesive book. She came with a fresh perspective of a wise person who is not familiar with the subject matter, but knows how to express ideas in a clear and readable manner. She knew how to present my Israeli reality in universal words. My gratitude and appreciation go to you, Geneva.

Last, but not least, I want to thank the many families I had the privilege of working with, over the years. Although the names throughout the book are fake, and the identity of the families is disguised, the examples are, nevertheless, based on the real stories. Each family was unique. Every family presented me with a new challenge, that enriched both my understanding and my tool kit. I am grateful to all my clients for the professional journey I made, and for the part of the path, each of them chose to walk along with me.

CHAPTER 1

Breaking the Silence

Worry weighs a person down; an encouraging word cheers a person up.

Proverbs, 12:25

Lucas stews at his desk, glaring at the company logo that bears his surname. He's just read an email from an old college buddy, the one who joined a tech start-up a week before graduation and is now on track for early retirement. Good for her. He's been working at the family business since summer break of his sophomore year, and even though he's given everything to the company, Lucas hasn't had a pay raise in *eight* years. His uncle is in charge, so the only people who float to positions of real responsibility are his cousins, regardless of how well they can do the job. *Never mind asking about stock in the company*, he muses. Holiday promises and deadline back-slapping had yet to bear meaningful fruit.

Nadia's mother founded their business with her brother, but now that both founders are looking seriously at retirement, there are terrible, itch-inducing questions about the future. Nadia had followed in her mother's footsteps, taking on more and more responsibility, until her homelife was in tatters and her office shelves were packed with plaques of appreciation. Neither of her cousins had joined the business, but if her mother and uncle sold it off, the profits would still be divided equally among them all.

Ken had always loved to cook, but in his family, working in the family business was just what you did. He appreciated his job—it had provided well for him and his children, and the extended family was tightly knit, often blending business retreats with family holidays—but he couldn't help but feel like he'd missed out on something crucial. If he left, would the family forget about him? When he was younger, he'd had dreams of attending a pastry school in Paris. Now, what with ten-hour work days and a forty-minute commute each way, he sometimes got to make dinner for his family on the weekends.

Fiona spent her MBA program relying on and trusting her compatriots, taking on new challenges and brainstorming new ideas in the company of other young people just as ambitious as she was. Now that she's home, learning the ropes of her family's business in the last few years before her father retires, she can't help but feel like her future seems smaller. The enterprise feels old-fashioned, the everyday issues of operation dull and humdrum. Fiona would never say so to her father, but she dreams of selling the business to a large corporation, or of going into an acquisition phase to accelerate growth.

Family businesses combine two already complex organizations and arrive at a situation so fraught with emotional complication that by the time they reach maturity, successors have often overcome personal and familial challenges that many people never even encounter—particularly since companies mature fast, technology changes constantly, and the possibilities can seem endless. Questions about choice and personal fulfillment, problems related to a domineering parent, efforts to introduce innovations in a company controlled by a successful but old-fashioned father, feeling inadequately rewarded for hard work, or the emotional and financial issues related to a position in a high-net-worth company—these aren't the sort of things successors can talk about easily. Being wealthy does not mean that life is simple, but every time a successor tries to acknowledge that fact, the response is knee-jerk. *How can you possibly feel lost or alone? You're RICH!*

But being rich comes with its own set of entirely valid, deeply human problems. Pretending they don't exist will only make them harder to solve.

THE SILENCE

I wrote this book because in my role as a family business continuity consultant, I've seen countless families struggle through all of these hard-to-articulate problems and fears. A common language between the successors and the family's senior generation is essential to creative family harmony, as is establishing common goals between siblings and cousins (whom we call *Gen Peers*), even if they've drifted apart in recent years. The tools and true stories you'll find in the rest of this book may inspire you to consider the way these issues affect your family. Building up your own leadership abilities and strengthening relationships with your Gen Peers and seniors may be the first step toward ensuring sustainable continuity for your family-owned business and, no less important, shoring up the integrity of your wider family unit.

Challenges to the integrity of your wider family unit are at the root of many of the problems faced by family-owned businesses. The absence of succession planning, in particular, is the sort of thing that leads to the problems experienced by Lucas, Nadia, Ken, and Fiona. Uncertainty, dissatisfaction, and a sense that one's work is unappreciated can all combine to make life in a family business simply miserable. But while trends in the business world and in personal dynamics are allowing more and more people to seek professional consultations in business planning and personal well-being, many families still resist planning for change.

Why?

The truth is that the future is frightening. Founders get old, death looms on the horizon, and nothing ever stays the same. Moreover, planning for the future causes past mistakes and covert feelings to surface. For some families, this is the greatest fear. As a result, it is easier to stick to the present and let urgent matters take priority over important ones. But succession planning *is* necessary. Avoiding it only kicks the issues down the road, meaning that they'll only land when the family is least capable of handling them. When a crisis erupts, finding solutions becomes much more difficult and *much* more expensive. It is better to "invest in peace," as a family member once told me. Doing so will help you to grow the family business—all while you foster family relationships and build a sense of personal fulfillment.

If you are a third- or fourth-generation successor, you've probably heard the saying, "First generation builds, second generation maintains, third generation destroys." My experience has taught me that while this may sometimes be true, the reasons behind it are more complex and far less deterministic than the idiom implies. Founders are, by definition, people who do not like systems, rules, or boundaries. They flourish on vagueness and flexibility. As one of them told me, "I love rules and respect them. But if they do not fit, I change them." The second generation lives with that vagueness, but less comfortably so. If they fail to establish the policies, structures, and procedures that did not exist until then, the coming generations are born into chaos. In these situations, it is only a matter of time until the organization disbands, a process that, as Ivan Lansberg notes, "constitutes a loss not only to the proprietary family, which often has most of its assets tied up in the firm, but also to the employees and surrounding community, whose economic well-being depends on the survival of the business."[1] This usually means working with a consultant.

You might be tempted to go the DIY succession planning route; however, consider this: running a business is an all-your-time enterprise. There's no developing an expertise in succession planning on the side. This is what consultants are *for*. Moreover, a third party can bring balance and clarity to what can be a very emotional and entangled discussion. A professional comes with a broad repertoire of up-to-date research and regularly refreshed statistics. They bring their experience of having seen many similar situations before. Admittedly, no two families are the same, so no solution is one-size-fits-all, but every family can be inspired by the solutions and successes of other families.

The unique challenges you face every day with a family business revolve around working together with your seniors and with your Gen Peers. They revolve around intergenerational partnership. With growing life expectancy, that partnership will necessarily grow ever longer. (I've already worked with several families in which three generations have run the business together.) At the same time, the mental and technological gap between generations seems to grow wider. This kind of partnership requires open dialogue, participatory leadership, rules, and structures. It may seem like putting off these institutions won't be that bad—surely a little unhappiness is inevitable, and eventually people grow to overcome their miseries? As one owner once told me, "My Prince Charles is not very happy, but Queen Elizabeth herself is very happy." But the truth is that this

---

1 Ivan Lansberg, "The Succession Conspiracy," *Family Business Review* 1, no. 2 (June 1988): 119–143.

kind of failure to act usually results in a complete lose-lose, in which the business suffers and family relations are ruined.

This book is about empowering successors to introduce necessary changes, and it is about doing so without disrupting family harmony and business growth.

WHY IS IT SO DIFFICULT TO BREAK THE SILENCE?

We're Special

The most common barrier to involving an outside expert in the family's problems is the notion that *our family is special*; that both the business and family problems are unique. *No one outside of my family could possibly understand our specific issues and personal histories*, successors think. *And the business itself is truly unparalleled, with dynamics and constraints that an outsider could never comprehend.* It's only after opening up about their interpersonal conflicts in workshops and seminars that the family begins to understand the systemic aspect of their situation. Eccentric Aunt Mary maybe isn't so odd—because she isn't a manager in the business, she only sees money through the lens of needing it for her household. But stingy Uncle Joe, on the other hand, is the CEO of the company, responsible for the continuous growth of the enterprise. He views reinvesting in the business as his utmost priority, so it makes sense that he'd hold back on distributing large dividends. When people shift from thinking that disagreements arise because of the individual family member to realizing that the conflict is a systemic issue, there is often a sigh of relief. *Oh, so we are not alone … other families have been through this and survived.* A clear-eyed understanding of all the different perspectives makes it much easier to discuss problems and find solutions.

Mental Spaghetti

To find a solution, a need must be clearly defined, but that is easier said than done. Simply being part of a family that owns a business can lead to an experience often referred to by my colleague, Tal Yahav, as "mental spaghetti," in which everything is mixed together: the money, the parent-child relationship, sibling rivalry, parental expectations, individual fulfillment, ambitions, dependency, work, salary, and whatever one's spouse thinks about the latest family vacation. All these things are tied up in one another. They are all dependent upon one another.

At this point, listening to the concerns of these family members can feel like watching 500 mixed-up pieces of a complex puzzle being poured on one's desk. Figuring out the way these concerns interlock is much like putting together that puzzle and finally revealing a larger picture. Once that picture is revealed, family members can begin to agree on what their reality is—not the subjective experience of one individual, but a shared reality that takes into account all the various perspectives and opinions. That full picture is what enables a family to stop and say, "Okay, so our challenge is . . ." before creating a tangible, organized plan, designed to achieve a specific solution.

It Might Explode

One challenge to this process is that family members often have the terrifying belief that by simply bringing up an issue, everything else will suddenly explode. For instance, out of respect for his father, a successor may fear speaking to him about his rudeness at the last manager meeting, but also, deep inside, that successor may feel that he hasn't brought sufficient value to the business, meaning that his father's rudeness is partially justified. He might think this way because, considering it's a family business, no one has ever taken the time to give him authentic feedback on his performance. He genuinely doesn't know whether or not his work is valuable. With all that anxiety in mind, the son may decide that it is just safer not to speak to his father about feeling hurt. Similarly, a young person might fear discussing his concerns about work with his mother because she may tell his father, which would cause problems at work. The fears and anxieties about speaking candidly are wild and varied, extending even in concerns that bringing up the issue of "who brought what" to the last family dinner might rekindle an old sibling rivalry about why one received the house and the other did not.

An employee at a non-family company may receive a bad review from their supervisor and then go home, have dinner with their family, and go to bed untroubled, as tomorrow is another day, and there's always a way to improve. But in a family business, that same poor review could translate directly into your father shouting at you in the middle of Sunday lunch. Telling your brother that you envy him could make it difficult to work together, meaning that one of you might have to find a job outside of the family business, which can in turn, cause financial stress, lack of security, and maybe even being "expelled" from the inner family circle. Simply airing a sibling rivalry (an otherwise common and natural phenomenon) can threaten one's entire lifestyle. All of these fears, and more, motivate family members toward little or no genuine communication on the most sensitive issues.

The solution they often take involves sweeping everything under the carpet and pretending that these issues do not exist. It is my job to put those issues on the table and to untangle the wires of the bomb, safely defuse it, and prevent it from exploding in the middle of the room. Afterward, I've had clients say to me, "You said that to my Dad? And the sky didn't fall in?" So far, the sky is intact.

Force of Character

Patriarchs themselves are another reason successors tend to keep silent, especially when those patriarchs are the founders of the enterprise. They are used to solving problems and they are used to doing so on their own. They see it as their duty, and everyone comes to them with problems. After all, this is what made them successful. Of course, they'll have the solutions.

But when they suddenly have to confront a complex emotional issue, such as a beloved daughter who wants to bring her less than qualified spouse to work in the family business, they may not have a clear-cut solution. And they might see that lack as a sign of weakness or incompetence. "Who am I, if I cannot solve this?" Better to keep silent. Better not to acknowledge the problem than to seem like someone without a solution.

I once worked with a family who lived on a high level of expenses. All family members (including second-generation spouses), lived happily off the company: salaries, house maintenance, insurance policies, computers, cell phones, etc. Everyone told me that there was plenty of money, and all was well. But the father, head of the business, was losing sleep at night. He had been summoned to the bank to discuss his dwindling personal resources and reconcile them to the soaring expenses. But he was the patriarch, the protector of all family members. He couldn't bring himself to reveal the bleak reality to his family, but he told *me*. And then I brought up the issue in a family meeting. There was a deep silence, but the sky did not fall, and the father was able to introduce a cost-cutting program for the entire family, which reintroduced economic sanity to the system.

Patriarchs often feel comfortable being the center of the family communication—the **solar system model** (see figure 1).

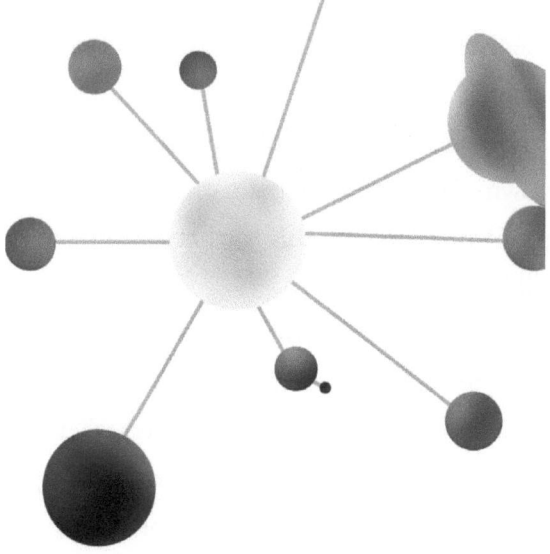

Figure 1. Solar system model

When I give lectures, I sometimes ask the audience, "Do any of your adult children ever have an opportunity to discuss serious issues among themselves in your absence? Not just 'Where are we going to spend the weekend?' but serious issues?" Almost always, no one raises a hand. This direct communication among Gen Peers generally does not arise until the parent is ill or actually passes away; however, by that time, learning to dialogue in order to solve conflicts becomes doubly difficult. I've found that promoting direct dialogue among Gen Peers is a manifestation of leadership and vision, as painful as it may be for the patriarch.

Not Real Problems

People often think that rich people's problems are not *real* problems. Society makes it unacceptable for rich people to discuss their issues or concerns. "What could you have to complain about? Not only do you have a lot of money, you also complain about it! Shame on you." But that doesn't mean that those issues just go away. The inability to express anxiety or fear about a person's situation—regardless of the way the situation compares to that of other people—inevitably results in a quiet isolation that creates impassable chasms between people. It fuels feelings of guilt and shame. Everyone, regardless of the contents of their wallet, needs an opportunity to discuss their concerns with someone they can trust and relate to.

WHY SHOULD THE SILENCE BE BROKEN?

That's Not Me

Mixing business and ownership with family life is a complex challenge. To ensure continuity, one must learn to manage complexity, rather than behaving as if reality was flat and simple. A patriarch once told me that he attributed his company's success to their global partnerships. He further explained that it was his ability to handle complex family situations that made him confident in his ability to manage complex international partnerships. "My family situation taught me how to bridge different perceptions, needs, and personalities. I then transferred these tools, reusing them to manage partners from different cultures and business mentalities."

One such bridge should cross the mental gap between first-generation founders and their successors. In an article published in the *Journal of Financial Planning*, "Immigrants and Natives to Wealth:

Understanding Clients Based on Their Wealth Origins," Grubman and Jaffe write, "Whether clients come to wealth during their lifetime or are raised with wealth from childhood broadly determines aspects of character, adjustment to wealth, identity, and family dynamics."[2] Even when they are wealthy, founders generally view themselves and their circumstances as poor. Because many started their business from scratch, there is a gap between the wealth they have in their minds and the wealth they have in their bank accounts. The second generation, on the other hand, is native to the land of wealth, and they hold very different perspectives on it. This creates a barrier that blocks understanding between these immigrant parents and their native children.

A client I worked with years ago was the founder of one of the most successful companies in Israel. His son, the successor, loved to cook, though this skill was unrelated to the family business. One day, the son went to his father and said, "Dad, I've registered for a course in vegetarian cooking."

The father replied, "Oh, that's a wonderful idea! We may not have enough money for meat." This was the founder of one of the largest companies in the country, but the fear that they may not have enough was a genuine anxiety. The gap between his self-perception and his bank account was difficult to bridge, meaning that it was impossible for him to understand his own children, who were raised with a sense of always having a safety net beneath them.

---

2   James Grubman and Dennis T. Jaffe, "Immigrants and Natives to Wealth: Understanding Clients Based on Their Wealth Origins," *Journal of Financial Planning* (July 2007): 46–54.

Tough Training

Soldiers of elite units everywhere in the world hear from their commanders the same rule: "Tough in training, easy in battle." This rule applies to families as well. Learning communication and conflict-resolution techniques is hard enough by itself, but when attempted during a time of emotional distress, it becomes almost impossible. Beginning the training in leadership and team work as early as possible allows for better coping mechanisms when the hard times come, while increasing the overall chance of success for the business and the family. Similarly, remuneration packages, procedures for the appraisal of the company's value, and rules of conduct in times of incapacitation should be established in times of "peace." If the family acquires the skills to communicate, to handle conflicts, and to reach agreements during a time of "training," they will be better equipped to handle decisions in times of economic or emotional stress.

CONCLUSION

Ideally, everything should be planned ahead of time, and transitions should be effortlessly smooth, but we do not live in an ideal world, and these ideals are rarely achieved. Families are usually triggered by some outside event, and the trauma of it pushes them to seek outside help. Once they begin to work with a professional, they find that discussing concerns alleviates feelings of frustration, guilt, shame, and hurt, which in turn solves many of the problems they were already experiencing.

For many clients, the reality of working with a consultant is similar to the experience of going on a hike and coming to a river or a mountain that you need to cross. You seek help from an experienced guide, and having crossed the river or mountain (and seeing how it was done), you can continue the journey on your own. By surmounting the obstacle in front of you, you are able to continue your trek—while also developing the tools that enable you to solve the next problem on your own.

I neither want nor need to be a crutch for a family to use every time they have to walk. I want to help families learn to walk on their own. My role is to remove obstacles and to teach people techniques and strategies that they can use in the future. By opening up channels of communication within families, family members will be able to honestly discuss issues amongst themselves the next time a difficult situation arises. By empowering successors to exercise their leadership, they will be able to introduce the innovations they see fit and be more competent in recruiting other family members along the way. This book has been designed to address the issues and concerns common to so many, while providing techniques and strategies to help successors and their families work through these difficult conversations themselves.

CHAPTER 2

My Experience Being in a Family Business

When I was young, a fire burned inside me, and I thought I could repair the whole world. When I grew up I despaired of repairing the world, and I thought about repairing my fellow townsmen. And when I realized that this was not possible either, I thought about repairing my family. And when I failed at this as well, I reached the conclusion that I must repair myself. After I had worked on myself, this in turn influenced my family, then all my fellow townsmen, and then the whole world.

Rabbi Chaim Halberstam of Sanz

Particularly in family-owned businesses, the paths of productivity and achievement are forged in family life. Our first exposure to teamwork comes from our siblings. A successor's dilemma—to stay or go—is rooted in a child's bond to their parents. The ability to distinguish your individuality through choices and independent thinking is fostered in early childhood, at your mother's knee. And the decision to consider yourself in relation to a larger entity—and still choose to follow your dreams—is identical to the way adult children must reimagine their role within a family.

CHILDHOOD

I was born in Israel in 1950 and raised in one of the newly formed kibbutzim, established in the formative years of the country, which relied on communal living. My home sat on a large plot of land, and we maintained a poultry farm, incubators, fields, and cowsheds. There were houses for the adults and separate houses for the children. I was an only child, but I lived and slept in one of the children's houses with a group of ten other children my age. We did everything together, from playing to chores to walking to and from the on-site kindergarten. That group was my world. (Looking back, I can easily identify them as my Gen Peers.)

To this day, I attribute my facility in sibling relations, team work, and collaboration to the lessons I learned from my time in the children's home. But my skill as a neutral third party also comes from that time. My situation was unusual. I was both part of a community and an outsider. I felt a sense of belonging with all the children I lived with, yet I didn't have any siblings of my own, as most of the other children did. And my family was decidedly different. My father spoke several different languages and often hosted foreign diplomats who wanted to gain an understanding of the structure of a kibbutz. I was one of the only children there who spoke a foreign language. These differences created a barrier between me and the other children that, at the time, saddened me. But today, I am able to understand and work with people of diverse backgrounds, cultures, and nationalities, while also maintaining a necessary level of objectivity when working within different family dynamics.

I chose not to return to the kibbutz as an adult, but I remain grateful for the experiences I received there, as they fostered many of the skills I built my career upon. Our particular kibbutz was still new, so we had very little money, and people worked very hard. The infrastructure was basic: no streetlights, and the roads were unpaved. My parents worked with the poultry and kept strange hours depending on hatching cycles. There was one evening, dark and cold, when both of my parents were working in the incubators. I woke up and needed them, in the way that only a frightened four-year-old needs her parents, so I set out for the farm, all by myself, and fell straight into a giant pothole that had filled with rainwater and mud. It was deep enough that I was stuck and couldn't get out, so I started to cry. A neighbor heard me and ran over, pulling me out of the mud, and to this day I think of that moment when I remember the kibbutz. That was the kind of environment I grew up in—one large family that lived, learned, and worked together.

My father had started the poultry farm, and both of my parents worked there, but the business belonged to the kibbutz, not to my parents. My father had a partner who managed the poultry farm with him, along with his wife. The pairing up of these two couples reinforced the sense of family that was so ingrained in the business. The rhythm of work and family, each tied up and supported by the other, has shaped my understanding of what family businesses can accomplish.

Through the lens of the poultry farm and my parents' relationship with each other and with their partners, I witnessed all of the struggles of a young business: competition, technological problems, regulatory problems, operations issues, and so on. These were the topics of conversation in my parents' home, which is why I understand the lack of boundaries between work and family life. For example, when the temperature fluctuated by one degree in the chick incubators, it would set off an alarm in my parents' home, and day or night, one of them would have to go to the farm and fix it.

The partnership between my father and his colleague taught me an important lesson about working partnerships. They were very different people, but their strengths complemented each other. They understood that it was okay to have weaknesses—they knew their partner could make up for them—so, in this sense, there was never any competition between them. Their relationship was built on complete trust. They respected one another and appreciated each other's unique strengths. My father was more intellectual and forward thinking; his partner was practical, with exceptional negotiation and sales skills. They shared a common goal and knew they could achieve anything if they worked together. Success is often achieved collaboratively, and the cornerstones of collaboration are *trust* and *respect*.

My father and his partner took joint responsibility for the poultry farm and driving the business forward. Prior to this, the kibbutz took in very little profit from the wheat and vegetables it harvested. What their partnership created in the poultry farm benefited everyone in the kibbutz. After building the poultry farm, they expanded into exporting and continued to grow the business from there. I should note that they didn't pretend to be experts in all aspects of growing this business—they hired professionals whose expertise was unambiguous. They brought in academic consultants, animal nutrition experts, electricians, and so on. They invested in their own knowledge, and that helped the business grow.

Even though they worked well together, my father and his partner didn't really connect on a personal level. My father's partner and his wife were Holocaust survivors who had arrived in the kibbutz directly from the concentration camps. They had experienced horrifying tragedies that my parents couldn't really understand. But these things were not up for discussion. Being so focused on building the future suited both of them well, each for his own reasons.

As a result, I learned about their traumatic history only as a young adult. For most of my childhood, I simply saw them as very trustworthy and industrious people who took on a lot of responsibility for the kibbutz. No one ever told me that they'd undergone such terrible loss—that wasn't the way people in the kibbutz thought. Everyone was focused on building the future.

In the kibbutz, the children started work very early. In the fourth grade, we'd finish school around noon, have lunch, and then go to work for two to four hours every day. We worked in the fields, the cowsheds, the chicken houses, the kitchen, or in the kindergartens. We did whatever was needed of us, wherever it was needed. As we grew, our hours increased. I learned what it meant to work hard from an early age, and I learned to work as a part of a team. It was a very idealistic, value-based, and future-oriented time.

AS AN ADULT

When I was twenty years old, I finished my military service and had to make a decision about whether I would return to the kibbutz and become a member or go my own way. I fretted for several days, but eventually I started thinking about how, if I returned to the kibbutz, my entire life would already be arranged for me. At the age of twenty-five, I would be sent to the university, and at the age of twenty-eight, I would be moved to a slightly larger apartment. At thirty, I would be entitled to new curtains. And at thirty-five, I might be entitled to a vacation overseas. This kind of certainty can be comforting, but for me, the idea that everything was already decided felt suffocating.

Though I disappointed many people at the kibbutz, I decided not to return. Going my own way meant, from that moment on, that I was on my own. This was both exciting and terrifying. It was a moment similar in tone to the dilemma of deciding whether or not to stay in a family business. There is a comforting security and familiarity in staying in the family business, and for many people, it doesn't necessarily feel like everything is preset. Even in a family business, you still have to prove yourself and pave your own way. But for others, it can feel the same way that returning to the kibbutz felt for me. Deciding against following the path that the world has set out for you—be it your family or the larger community—carries a risk of upsetting the people you care about. But it doesn't mean that those people are out of your life. I've long maintained relationships with the people who shaped my childhood. In fact, this month I am going back to celebrate the ninetieth birthday of the widow of my father's business partner.

After my military service, I went to Jerusalem, got a job, and registered to study at the university. It was then that it dawned on my father that he could not help me at all. Everything he had belonged to the kibbutz. This was never a problem for me—I had assumed from the get-go that I'd be pursuing this ambition on my own—but I realized quickly that this was a devastating fact for my parents. Parents want to give to their children, sometimes more than the children want to receive. It's not just about protecting the people they love. For many parents, providing for their children is justification for their years of hard work. This is particularly true when the hard work comes at the expense of spending time and energy with those children as they grow.

In Jerusalem, I earned my undergraduate degree in psychology and education. I then went on to earn my master's degree before traveling to the United States with my husband for my PhD in counseling. My parents didn't understand my decision to study psychology. At the time, I didn't know what I wanted to do with my career and chose to study psychology simply because it was challenging and competitive. There are people who, from an early age, know exactly what they want to do with their lives. I was not one of these fortunate people. I belong to the group of people who don't have a clear calling but end up integrating several disciplines and creating a new vocation. I should have expected that my career would follow this path. After all, my father had a PhD in philosophy, was an ordained rabbi, a scholar of art history, and a specialist in poultry nutrition and genetics. I wound up with a vocation that combines psychology, system theory, business, and law.

I finished my PhD and then stayed in the United States to teach in the education department at the university, all while conducting research in the field of community health sciences. When I returned to Israel, I began management consulting because I was able to use my psychology skills in a business-oriented environment. I enjoyed the work, and did it for years, until I was asked to provide consultation services for a family business.

One of the largest food industries in Israel is owned and operated by a very unusual family. The business had begun in a small cowshed, but by the time I started consulting for them, the operation had grown to span the whole country and was run by the second generation—a brother and sister. One day, the sister said to me, "You seem to be a good consultant. We're starting to set up a plan for the transition to the third generation if you want to work with us on that."

That was how I began succession planning for family businesses. Two years later with Dr. Orenia YanaiI, we started a consulting firm dedicated to family business planning. Our partnership lasted more than fifteen years. Together we built our methodology and our reputation. We were very different in character and style, but we shared values and enthusiasm, which enabled us to create a working partnership that served as a role model for many of our clients. When it was time to part ways, we decided to walk our talk and separate amicably.

WORK AND PRIVATE LIFE

I have been consulting for family businesses for more than twenty years now, and my personal life has always shaped my understanding of the work I do. For my entire career, I've seen my personal life reflected back in the struggles of my clients. When I look at the relationship I have with my husband Hillel, for instance, I see a conversation based on love and cemented in common values, shared goals, and deep trust—all of which are things every family business *needs* in order to find and keep success. My husband and I respect each other and our separate careers, and because we have that mutual respect, we've been able to support each other through differences of opinion, disappointments, careers pulling us in opposite directions, and the ever-shifting requirements of raising a family while pursuing our careers.

Admittedly, I bore the brunt of that last challenge. For many women, their femininity and ties to family can lead to their being undervalued in the work place. I never thought of myself that way. I was an only child, so I was never in danger of feeling less important than a boy, and my parents named me for the biblical Tamar, who stood up to Judah and proved him wrong. Jewish tradition suggests that as a reward for her righteousness, her line was the one that birthed King David. My father used to say that she was the world's first feminist, and my being named after her said a lot about the hopes he and my mother had for me. But for all that internal confidence, combining a career and family life was still a challenge. I found that the mix required me to stretch and flex in a multitude of different ways as my children grew up, and even with all the respect my husband had for the situation, there was no clear answer to the difficulties inherent in combining career and family. This sad state of affairs does not seem to have changed much in recent years. As they raise their own kids, my children are facing the same challenges.

But beyond the difficulties imposed by an unequal world, the respect and trust between my husband and me kept our partnership solid and helped us navigate these rough waters together. And to a significant extent, the two-way interaction between my family and my professional life allows me to have greater insight into the issues and concerns that challenge my clients.

For instance, in my conversations with the senior generation, I sometimes say, "Let me change hats now and talk to you as parent to parent." This always catches their attention and gives me a moment to share a few insights and experiences that they probably recognize from their own lives. And then I can switch back and, from the perspective of a colleague, I can ask them to revisit their attitudes and to reconsider old issues with "new eyes."

On the one hand, I am a mother of three and a grandmother of two. As a mother, I am not a psychologist or a consultant. I behave like any other mother: I get upset, I lose my temper, I have expectations of them that often do not match their wishes and aspirations, and I do everything a normal mother and grandmother does. But my practice gives me a different perspective, one that prompts me to reconsider my attitudes toward my children's choices. I don't believe there's any sense in firmly partitioning my work life from the life I share with my family, particularly because I find that my family life enriches the emotional spectrum I can bring into my encounters with other families.

For example, I learned from my son to listen without trying to solve the problem. When my son was in the beginning of his military service in the air force, he was placed in a unit that he hated. He called me with a barrage of complaints about his commander and the guys in the unit. He felt that his work was of no value. Everything was terrible. At the time, I knew several people in the air force, and I immediately said, "Son, do you want me to call the commander of the air force? The deputy commander?" I mentioned a lot of big names, and my son was quiet for a moment. Then he said, "Mom, I just wanted you to hear me." That was a lesson for life.

In July 1997, my nephew, Captain Nadav Milo, the son of my husband's only brother, was killed in action while commanding his special ops unit. The tragedy shook the entire family, and it led to my husband and me becoming much more aware of our civic responsibilities. Years later, that civic engagement has become deeply entwined in our lives, and we've found that weaving strands of social responsibility through both our personal and professional lives has enriched both areas. Armed with this personal experience, I am quick to draw the issue of social responsibility to the attention of every client I work with. I've found that the younger generation is usually already aware of it and eager to transform this interest into a shared family value and integrate it into the family's collective agenda. My personal life taught me that giving is enriching in itself, and the bonds created through the context of giving stand the test of time and crisis.

Similarly, being a mother taught me that I shouldn't think that I know what is best for someone else, even for my own children. For example, all three of my children made choices early on that I thought were wrong choices. My son dropped out of school in the tenth grade—something that, in my eyes, was an awful decision. At the time, I was devastated, certain that he'd turned his back on education and progress. But if you see him today, you'll find that he's working on his PhD in electronics engineering. Somewhere along the way, he made up for leaving school. Regardless of what I thought, he knew what was best for him.

I voiced my opinion each time one of my children made choices I disagreed with. But, in retrospect, I'm sure that they made the choices that were right for them at the time. My view of "the right thing" is not necessarily the right thing for them. This is especially important to keep in mind when children decide not to join the family business, which is always a possibility. Even though parents think they know what is best for their children, it is better to listen to what young people say their desires and opinions are. By valuing the perspectives of others and allowing an empathetic approach to relationships within a family business, we can create opportunities for growth and creativity that would not have existed otherwise. The personal and the professional must go hand-in-hand.

CHAPTER 3

Why Your Family Must Dare to Ask the *Why* Questions

*And it will come to pass if your children say to you,
What is this service to you?*

Exodus, 12:26

Strange things end up on the Seder table. Parsley and salt water, hard-boiled eggs and unleavened bread—everything displayed with ceremony. The first year I was old enough to recognize the custom, I turned to my parents to ask, "Why? Why is *that* on the table?" You won't get a four-year-old to sit quietly and listen to the story of Exodus unless they want to hear it. By provoking the question, my parents had ensured that I would listen to the answer.

Questions and answers make up a big part of my practice. I usually begin consulting with a family business by holding a meeting with the entire family. I speak generally about family businesses and common dilemmas, and I tell families that the main goal is for everyone to leave the room with a lot of new questions. Answers can come later; new questions are the goal for now.

For most successors, the questions that leap to mind are things like, *When shall I become independent? How does being wealthy affect my life? What does it mean to be an owner? Does my brother receive more/less than me?* And finally, *Am I willing to make the family business my career, or do I just want to be involved as the owner, leaving the day-to-day work to someone else?* These are crucial questions, but their answers rely on the answers to other yet more essential questions—questions I call the *why* questions. These can be questions, such as, *Why did this business survive the passage of time and changes? Why are we rich? Why do people around us expect from us what they expect? Why do I want to be part of this?* And, *Why should we stay together?*

Why questions get to the heart of what we value and how we see the future, but they also seem to be the questions that, for a lot of people, often go unasked. Asking these questions can be uncomfortable—they can force you to rethink your own perspective, maybe even doubt yourself—but the value in doing so outweighs that discomfort. Our worldviews drive our choices, and we cannot productively relate to each other until we understand those perspectives.

We once worked with a family who had not grown up with the wealth their father had acquired. The wealth became known to them only when they were adults. For years, they related to the wealth as something that belonged exclusively to their father and believed that they could go about their lives as if the wealth had nothing to do with them. When it came time to think about how they would assume responsibility for this wealth and how they would prepare the third generation, they suddenly had to begin asking the *why* questions. *Why were they rich? Why did the wealth affect their lives the way it did? Why did they want to stay together?*

These successors had to figure out for themselves what they thought should be done with the wealth their father had accumulated. And they had to know why, specifically, they felt the way they did.

These are tough questions. There are no easy answers. But the siblings were courageous and did not back off. They ended up deciding that the money itself didn't matter as much as what they could accomplish with it. What they wanted to accomplish was to build up their parents' legacy by using the wealth to contribute to the community. They realized that they could accomplish more by staying together, and that's what they did. It was only through careful self-examination and reflection upon their shared values and differences that they were able to come to that answer and find it satisfying. This paved the way for the creation of a Family Mission Statement, that was an inspirational document meant to last for generations to come.

We had another case where the dilemma was even more complex. Sharon and Dean inherited Sharon's father's business after his sudden death. The couple wanted to manage the wealth effectively and responsibly, but a conflict between their values and their financial interests immediately appeared: the stream of income was derived from business activities that they strongly disapproved of. To make matters worse, that same stream of income had enabled Sharon's father to support the rest of the extended family, which meant that Sharon's relationships with her family were now entwined with what for Sharon was a morally dubious income stream.

An in-depth conversation with Sharon and Dean made it clear that while they wanted to accept the wealth her father had left them, they had to carefully sort through the values that guided him, in order to adopt those that they could live with. One such value was to maintain their relationships with Sharon's family. By asking the tough *why* questions, they discovered that they had to gradually and responsibly shift to a new business direction, in order to preserve the wealth and maintain the familial relationships that depended on the old income stream. Not an easy task. The couple is currently working on gradually shifting the direction of the business, so as to better align it with their values. Their relationships with the extended family will have to be revisited later.

WHO SHOULD ASK *WHY*?

Founders have a vision. They've been working toward it for years. They have a goal that makes them get up in the morning and do what they do. They already know the answers to the *why* questions. For them, the real answer is often "because I have to make a living to survive." The second generation, however, is usually not in survival mode. They usually don't have the same passion for the founder's work, so the *why* questions are more pertinent to them. These questions become even more significant as the business moves into the hands of the third and fourth generations. Each individual successor chooses between working in the family business and following a different path. In either case, they should know *why* they made that choice. They should interrogate their motivations and come to understand the worldview that drives their impulses. It is not enough to blindly follow in a parent's footsteps.

UNDERSTANDING THE FEAR

There are a lot of fears around money—increased responsibilities, expectations that the wealth should be used "properly" (a word whose meaning often lacks actionable definition)—and it is easy to be intimidated by the sudden onslaught of decisions and obligations.

Sometimes, successors decide not to remain in the family business. In most of these cases, they stay on as owners, or future owners, and decide not to actively work in the family business. But stepping away can be frightening—for both successors and founders. Being in the family business is not just about having a job; it's also about belonging to the family.

The possibility of losing this connection can be overwhelming, and being on the outside of the business can be scary. From being left out of dinner conversations to watching previously loving relationships with family members wither, the stakes are deeply personal and tied to a successor's sense of worth and identity. Questions like, *If the family vacation is partly a business retreat, will I still be invited if I don't work in the business?* or *Will my children have an opportunity to work in the business if I leave?* are all valid concerns. They may be answered through discussions, family rules, and appropriate mechanisms.

But more importantly, these anxieties shouldn't dictate the entirety of a successor's career. Coping with the fear requires going back to exercising the choice muscle and taking responsibility for what comes of it. I have seen young men and women who continued to work in the business—even though they did not like it, did not want to be there, and were objectively not very good at the job—just because the rules of what they would be entitled to once they left were not clear. Staying in a situation you hate just because you don't know what'll happen if you leave is terrible for your peace of mind. It will leave you sad and bitter. It's usually pretty bad for the business as well.

This kind of self-analysis is harder than it sounds. We are naturally drawn to the familiar, even when we know its pitfalls, and it can feel easier to live a life unfulfilled than risk disappointing one's parents or rocking the boat of financial comfort. Every family has its own quirks, its own perspective. Staying in the family business means that a successor can deal with familiar problems using familiar methods. It can feel simpler than striking out for new territory.

There is a story about a rabbi in a poor community who grew tired of his people's constant complaints about their troubles and misfortunes. One day, he told them that they could put their troubles in sacks and bring them to his house. With all the sacks gathered in his living room, the rabbi shuffled them up, and let each person take home someone else's sack. After three days, they were all banging on his door, asking to be given back their own sack. The rabbi had shown them how one's familiar troubles may be preferable to the unfamiliar troubles of someone else.

Is there a combination? A way for successors to have a sack of troubles that are both familiar enough to feel safe and new enough to feel significant? Every so often, I come across successors who want to be in the business but also want to make changes to it. This group has its own set of anxieties. Say a successor identifies a need for a new IT system in the family business. It may improve processes and create greater efficiency, but it costs $8 million. Does the successor make that change? Is he willing to deal with the consequences? Change carries risk, and if a successor has chosen to stay in their parent's business, the risk of failure is more than monetary: it puts at stake the successor's family relationships, self-esteem, and heritage.

Successors sometimes get around the fear of failure by passing it back to their parents: "Let Dad make the decision; it's his company, after all." But this strategy becomes increasingly burdensome. How much responsibility would you deliberately heap on your parent's shoulders? And what if he opposes your plan? In one case, the successor stowed the idea, a pipedream for another life, and instead talked about how he would have to leave the family business to make that dream happen, even though the truth was that it had nothing to do with the business itself. This successor avoided risks because he feared failure. No matter where he went, from one business to another, he would always carry that fear with him. In this case, the solution was not to leave the family business, but rather to develop leadership, competence, and self-confidence.

For some people, this fear of failure arises from inexperience in making choices. If you've grown up affluent, chances are your experience choosing between one course of action and another is very different from that of your parents. Founders take risks and make difficult decisions to create a successful business. Simply by being native to affluence, many successors have not been in situations that mandated risk and personal choice.

You can't get comfortable with making high-risk decisions without a lifetime of practice making choices. Practicing decision-making can start small: Do I buy jeans or two t-shirts? Should I go to the movies or save for vacation? As unobtrusive as it can be, this kind of mental strength is a skill that kids need to learn. We've developed a program to teach affluent parents to encourage their teenage children to make choices and manage their own budget. We've focused on building this skill at an early age so that by the time the kids reach adulthood, they understand how to weigh their options, make decisions, and accept the consequences.

But inexperience isn't the only thing that prompts successors to pass the buck. The sad truth is that blaming your situation on someone else feels safer than assuming responsibility. If you've spent your whole career dreaming of trying something new, and not doing it, you might not know that it's fear of failure that has kept you down. You might be blaming the business, or your parents, or your siblings for somehow preventing you from acting. I've had clients say, "I cannot make the change because Dad would not let me," or "My brother doesn't think that the bottom line can bear the expense. He is crazy. He is dominant." This kind of buck-passing isn't conscious. We genuinely believe that our opportunities are limited by our family members or the business.

Eilon was 35 years old when I met him. His father had chosen him to take over the business, and he'd given up a struggling career as an independent architect. His father was not healthy and the succession needed to happen quickly, but Eilon never saw himself as having control over the business—or even his own actions. He felt and acted like a victim of the situation, despite the fact that he had *chosen* to join the family business. He couldn't take responsibility "because the sales manager didn't show up on time." He couldn't approach new customers "because Father wouldn't let me." And so on. It took several months of work to slowly change Eilon's perspective, and while he still occasionally reverts to this victim mentality, overall, he understands that he is his own agent, and the only one stopping him from fulfilling his dreams is him. The real-world situation has not change, but his attitude has, and that's what made the most difference to his overall satisfaction.

TAKING RESPONSIBILITY

Changing the way we think is a big step and it takes a long time, but the benefits of doing so can be seen almost immediately. Once we stop blaming other people or external circumstances, we change our entire perspective. For example, my husband and I lived and worked in the United States for several years. We enjoyed our lives there, but we wanted to return to Israel. Because it was our choice to return, we don't complain about the country. It's not that we can't complain—we don't feel indebted or behooved to keep quiet—and the things we could complain about are numerous:

- My politics don't match the government's.
- It's a small country with limited opportunities.
- Traffic is overwhelming.
- The cost of living is high.

But returning was our decision. I am not a victim. My perspective is one in which I can always do something to make my experience better.

In family businesses, there's a tendency to pass responsibility back to our parents and blame them for our failures. They accomplished the herculean effort of raising us to adulthood; they brought the enterprise to where it is; they're the most responsible people we've ever known. So, they are also the blame for any mistake or wrongdoing we observe. And certainly, they are not perfect! This way of thinking may be true, but it ignores several important realities. I often find myself telling the successors of family businesses that every parent tries to do the best they can, but they can give their children only what they have to give. Some parents have a lot of love and attention to lavish on their kids, but lack financial resources. Other parents have a lot of money, but no time to spend going to ball games or driving the carpool. Regardless of what you got from your parents, you should know that it was everything they had. Blaming them for not spontaneously growing extra energy or abilities or money for your sake only feeds into you feeling like a victim. If you want your circumstances to change, passing responsibility for your dreams along to your parents will not help. The only thing that will eventually satisfy you is a shift in your own attitude, toward assuming responsibility for your own path.

And really, this kind of change applies beyond personal satisfaction. We once had a client complain that her father wouldn't listen to her idea for the business. We asked if she'd tried to present the idea in a way that was clear to her dad—maybe he was a person who only looks at Excel sheets or business plans—because the truth was, she couldn't change how her dad works, thinks, or makes decisions, but she *could* change the way she worked with him so that he engaged with her ideas. If you can move from an attitude in which the world must accommodate you to one in which you shift to meet the world halfway, you're much more likely to see success.

DIFFICULT CHOICES

If it isn't fear, it's probably genuine confusion. We all draw from a constantly replenishing well of other people's expectations and societal responsibilities, all of which can present as reflections of our true desires. To sort the wheat from the chaff, I recommend writing out those thoughts. For instance:

1. *My parents' expectations are high, and I don't want to disappoint them, as they love me so much.*
2. *Since I was five years old, Dad has said that I would take over the business. There is no one else to fill my place if I leave.*
3. *Right now, I am financially secure and Dad recently bought our new house. But my wife is about to have our second child. I cannot afford to leave now.*
4. *I don't know if I'll inherit any of my parents' wealth if I'm not around to fight for my fair share.*
5. *But ... I really want to be a violinist.*

Once the list is complete, it can be shared with your Gen Peers, who might have put into words something that existed in you as well, even if you weren't aware enough of it to write it down yourself.

When all the lists have been put together, they can be examined and the sorting process can begin. In other words, examine these sometimes contradictory thoughts, evaluate them one at a time, and weigh them carefully against reality and possible courses of action.

Such exploration often involves looking at one's motivations. Motivations are key in making choices and commitment. Let's consider how our motivations appear in the picture. We can start with the motivation that is triggered by parents. Being needed is oftentimes a powerful enough motivator to change the fate of a family business. I once worked with an Israeli high-tech entrepreneur who had been very successful with several start-ups, but one of his companies was stuck because of a technological problem. He turned to his son, who had recently graduated from the Technion in Israel, and asked if he would look into the problem. The father told him, "If we don't find a solution, I shall have to close down the company." The son accepted the challenge, managed to find the solution, and revitalized the company. Now, fifteen years later, the company is traded on Nasdaq, the son is the CEO, and the father is the chairman of the board. The father's need was the compelling reason for the son's choice. Need was enough.

The four Mazuz siblings had gathered for a two-day retreat to discuss continuity in their family business. They were all in their twenties, and they were all at the beginning of their respective career paths. At the outset, it seemed that all four of them were vying for the right to work in the business, although their mother had reported that none of them were interested. So, we set up an exercise that looked at why each one wanted to participate in the business and made those motives public to the rest of the siblings. They all compared notes, and the results were eye-opening. One of them wanted to be there just because she'd always competed with the rest of her siblings, and she needed to win. Another wanted to be there to be close to Dad. A third relished the financial security derived from working for the family business. The fourth, contrary to his mother's perception, was actually interested in the subject matter and the business activities of their specific enterprise. After we'd brought these motivations to light, the siblings were able to look at the situation more logically and less emotionally. The one sibling who really liked the subject matter was happy to go to work in the business, but the other three were able to say to themselves, "That's not a good enough foundation to build my career on." The process of understanding what it is that you really want is difficult to do alone, but it is essential.

SIBLINGS

It doesn't take a lot of digging to discover that many successors base their decisions on sibling rivalry. Sibling rivalry shows up in a multitude of situations, whether you're the chosen heir, feeling threatened by a brother who wants your position, or you're angling for the heir position and your sister stands in your way. Perhaps you never knew that you wanted to be part of the business, but as soon as your dad settled on passing it to your brother, you suddenly needed to get involved. Or maybe you just wanted to prove your abilities to your mom and being in the business was the best way to prove it to her. Familial relationships are often at least as important to a successor as whether or not they enjoy working in the family business. Maintaining these relationships may well be a good enough motivation, as long as you understand that that's why you're staying in the business and you know that you deliberately made that choice.

When it comes to succession planning for families, I like to hold a sibling workshop, similar to the one we conducted with the

Mazuz siblings. It is a two-day workshop to develop communication, explore common values, and deepen the siblings' understanding of their responsibilities as future owners. Doing it together lays the foundation for a working partnership. Siblings mostly just remember each other as children, so bringing them back together as adults is a good way to let them acquaint each other with the responsible, active people they've become. They become peers you can rely on, rather than the annoying little kids who followed you everywhere and kept you from doing the really fun stuff. These relationships are valuable, and once we learn how crucial they are, and make room for the grown-ups we have all become, we're able to make joint decisions that more closely reflect what we really want.

VALUES

Identifying common values within the family and the business (i.e., the foundation for creating sustainable continuity) can only be done by earnestly asking oneself and one's family the deepest, heaviest *why* questions.

I met Shawn at a NextGen seminar I conducted for an international bank. Little did I know that he would propel that seminar into a wide-scale process with his family. Shawn was the eldest grandchild of the founder of a large consumer products company. The founder and his wife still owned all the shares, while their son and daughter ran the business. The third generation comprised the cousins who were all interested in eventually becoming responsible owners of the family business, but tensions between the cousins' parents began to divide them, and the question *Why should we stay together?* was forever a forethought.

As a practical person with a strong business orientation, Shawn tried to avoid the heavy *why* questions. He identified several areas regarding governance that needed to improve and decided to start with that, but it was through exploring those areas that he ran into the family's central problem. His grandfather, the founder, despite the company's success and his family's growth, continued to run the family as he had when they were one nuclear family and the business was a start-up. He told family members what to do based on what he believed their strengths were. If one of his children or grandchildren understood finance, he asked them to take care of the insurance. If another was experienced in real estate, he told that person to obtain the city permits. And so on. The situation didn't sit well with anyone. There was a lack of clear direction in each role, and the family members either received compensation that was disproportionate to their work, or they were not compensated at all.

Shawn decided to recruit his siblings to tackle the issue. Together, they started talking about the chaotic situation. It was up to the third generation to be the ones to create policies and to show the way to implementing necessary changes. They decided to put together a proposal for a formal Family Agreement and to present it to their parents. It was at this point that the siblings raised the question of *Why stay together?* and decided to invite their cousins to participate in the process.

The first few facilitated meetings of the entire third generation dealt primarily with the *why* questions. First, they identified their values—personal and shared—and the facilitated encounter became a safe space to allow them to voice their fears, including issues of inferiority and superiority between the branches, and their concerns about a future together. These were difficult conversations, in which they laid out the fear that the two branches of the family might not get along and would eventually need to separate. After working through these *why* questions together and strengthening the familial bonds sparked in childhood, they figured out that their values were compatible enough to let them work together, in spite of their differences. This was the foundation for the Family Agreement.

Working from that base of shared values and transparent motivations, they began to codify fair and equitable rules regarding who is eligible to work in the business, who makes the hiring decisions, how salaries and promotions are determined, and so on.

The entire family convened for the presentation of the proposed family organizational chart. Along with the changes, the cousins presented the need for a board of directors with representatives from both the second and third generations. Because the second and third generations held similar values, the second generation was easily able to accept the work that the third generation had put into defining the rules that would govern the family's business dealings.

I've also worked with families who don't apply a values conversation to their business. Their business exists for the sole purpose of making money. This can be a driving force during the survival stage of the business, but when the enterprise grows and becomes stable, usually around the time when successors join the business, money cannot provide a driving force. Once survival is secured, money loses its motivational efficacy. Money is a result of good work—not the driving force behind it. People are driven by a cause that relates to their values, and if the family is only in business for the money, something crucial is lacking.

An honest recognition of values—both individual and collective—is essential for a business to be innovative and sustainable over time. You cannot work toward a goal if you don't know what that goal is.

CONCLUSION

A psychologist or a therapist might tell someone, "If you're not happy in your job, leave. Go somewhere else," which is probably the right thing to say to someone who is an employee in a non-family business. With a family business, things are more complex.

The choice of whether to separate from a family business is difficult and multifaceted. It takes self-reflection and hard conversations with family members. Due to the complexity involved, I believe it is best to be guided by an impartial professional who understands the complexity of the family business and can facilitate greater introspection. By taking on these issues now, by asking the *why* questions and earnestly seeking the answers, you can find clarity and direction, both as an individual and as a group. Commitment is the natural consequence of a choice made with clarity.

There's a fear that asking these questions will negatively affect family relations, but more often than not, we find that it eventually solidifies the family's impulse to band together. Dealing with these questions lets family members feel that their unity has a solid foundation of honesty and genuine self-knowledge, rather than false agreement borne out of fear of loss.

Making choices and answering the *why* questions are important steps in succession planning. Gradually, a successor must make the transition to being a responsible owner, which means understanding the business, being able to make decisions, and knowing how to manage the people who deal with the wealth. These skills rely on having a sincere, honest relationship with yourself, and knowing what you want and why you want it. You cannot be a responsible owner—someone who is accountable to the business, the family, and the community—if you're at all unclear on who you are and how you're shaped by your values.

CHAPTER 4

Making the Younger Generation the Catalyst for Change

One man was walking through a desert and who was hungry, tired, and thirsty. And he found a tree whose fruits were sweet and whose shade was pleasant, and a stream of water flows beneath it. He ate from the fruits of the tree, drank from the water in the stream, and sat in the shade of the tree. And when he wished to leave, he said: Tree, tree, with what shall I bless you? If I say to you that your fruits should be sweet, your fruits are already sweet; if I say that your shade should be pleasant, your shade is already pleasant; if I say that a stream of water should flow beneath you, a stream of water already flows beneath you. Rather, I will bless you as follows: May it be God's will that all saplings which they plant from you be like you.

Talmud, Taanit 5b

Friday night dinner is sacred. Maybe not *technically*—there's no holy text that proclaims the sanctity of the meal itself—but it's the beginning of the Shabbat weekend. And in Israel, that means it's time for the entire family—parents, children, and grandchildren—to come together and strengthen the bonds that keep the family whole.

Throughout—and because of—our long history of diaspora and persecution, we as a people have not had one governmental authority that was willing or able to justly regulate our communities as a whole. We have had to rely on family structures and local community support, and our family ties therefore look more like a collaborative arrangement than a hierarchy of commands and obedience. We have never had a *You're only responsible for yourself* mentality. Parents have long recognized that in order to ensure the best future for their families, they need to continue supporting their children well into adulthood. Grandparents, who often feel responsible for maintaining traditions, happily take a hand in raising their grandchildren, and after parents pay off the mortgage on their own house, they take on another loan to help their children pay for *their* homes. The mentality behind these sacrifices is clear: *We're in this together.*

This enmeshed family culture and lack of formality is the kind of environment that fosters innovation. Innovation appears when there are no set rules and one has to create his or her own rules and invent a new reality. Creativity cannot be bound to strict rules or authority, or to an obsession with maintaining the status quo. It must be free to build and revise, regardless of whether a rule has worked for thousands of years. When a rule no longer fits the community, the community must change that rule.

This is why the younger generation's integration into the family business inevitably requires or drives change, and it's why we see so much conflict centered around the difficulties inherent in doing so. We tell our children to be creative, to innovate and explore and reinvent, but when it comes time to blend their ideas with an existing organization, we balk at the feeling that their enthusiasm for change might be applied to *our* life's work.

I try to balance these two forces. My work is to enable a harmonious blend between tradition and formality on one hand, and innovation and change on the other.

CREATING CHANGE

I used to think that if the senior generation did not want to work to integrate the younger generation into the business, there wasn't much anyone could do about it. For several years I operated under the belief that the younger generation could never effect change unless the senior generation supported it.

Around twenty years ago, I worked with a family whose father held the reins of the company pretty tightly. His two adult sons worked in his business, and both felt unfulfilled and frustrated because their father wouldn't let them do anything on their own. One of the brothers wanted to throw a party for his son's bar mitzvah, but he didn't have the money to do so unless he got it from his father. This man was about fifty years old, and the party he wanted to throw was not unreasonably extravagant, but the salary he drew from his father's company was still not enough to cover it, and he had to ask him for the money.

I told the father that this arrangement was unhealthy for everyone involved, and he replied that he had never refused his son money and didn't see anything wrong with the situation. The more I argued with him, the tighter he clung to his authority. I stepped away from the family when it became clear that regardless of his stated desires, the father was not truly willing to allow any sort of transition to the next generation to take place. I felt strongly at the time that such a change had to come from the family's patriarch.

If the same thing happened to me now, however, I would probably say, "Well, the father doesn't want to be part of the transition, but the younger generation can still think about how they'll one day assume responsibility for the company." They can recruit the older generation into this process, even if the senior generation is not interested in initiating change. The successor has a significant role to play in effectively planning for business continuity—indeed, both senior and junior generations have a responsibility to involve themselves in this process. So long as it's clear that continuity is about a partnership between the generations, rather than a replacement of one generation by the other, respectful relationships can continue to thrive while the senior generation gradually moves from management roles to board positions. As elders, their influence on the family and the business comes from giving guidance and sharing wisdom, while the management responsibilities should gradually move into the hands of the younger generation.

Continuity planning all comes down to enabling partnership and communication between generations. When both generations can discuss issues openly and listen to different viewpoints, they are able to make joint decisions that ensure a successful future. Without this open communication, lasting continuity will probably not happen.

THE SENIOR GENERATION

I've found that the founding or managing generation is often eager to hand over some of the burden of control. Even when everyone around them describes them as dominant and centralistic, they insist that they will happily release control as soon as they are sure that someone else can properly take hold of it. I have learned to believe them! In many cases, the patriarch can't believe that anyone can properly replace them. But under the right circumstances, I have seen even the most centralistic patriarchs release control—as long as they were sure that the next generation could cope. Most members of the senior generation understand that they can't do everything and it's important to let the younger generation try things and reinvent the business when the time comes. There always comes a point when the continuing success of the family business depends on the next generation.

A patriarch once approached me upon returning from a trade show in the United States. He explained that while he was in his booth, his most important client had come to him and said, with great sorrow, that he was leaving him. "I have been here year after year," the client had said. "You are always here alone, without a successor. I cannot base my business on a supplier who does not have a successor." The patriarch took this to heart and immediately began the process of preparing his son to manage the company.

However, patriarchs often know only one way to maintain control: their way! The task of proving to them that the success of the business can be properly built in a variety of different ways is up to the next generation. I've found that patriarchs have to be "recruited" into the change process by their children.

THE YOUNGER GENERATION

Even if control is in the senior generation's hands, and even if the younger generation doesn't have the power or authority yet, their commitment and involvement in the business gives them the influence to effect change. The next generation is the future, and that makes it possible for them to reinvent the business.

Rachel, Ari, and Lia invited me to a "blind date" in a coffee shop in Tel Aviv. The only thing I knew about them was that they belonged to the Grambar family, a multi-generational, multi-branch family, with large business enterprises in Israel. I met three young people (between the ages of twenty-nine and thirty-seven), each of whom was building his or her career separately from the family business. Rachel had recently returned from a three-day seminar on governance in family business, in Europe, and was looking for a way to jump-start an initiative within her own family. The three made it clear that their parents were not concerned and did not think their children needed to do anything about continuity. "Don't worry, we have enough money to let you do whatever you want," was the message they heard from the senior generation. Yet, the successors were curious. They felt ambivalent about the business, the wealth, their future roles as owners, and perhaps most crucially, the connections between them. "There are nineteen of us in the successor generation, but we don't really know one another," said Lia. "I've got cousins I would barely recognize on the street."

At the end of our first meeting, they knew that they wanted to explore something with regard to their future role as successors, but they needed professional help to better define it. The next step was a series of one-on-one conversations with each of the nineteen fourth-generation members. This allowed me to hear the range of voices, needs, and desires that existed in the group. It also caused them to "wake up" to their unique situation and to pose new questions to themselves. After my colleague and I had completed that first round of talks, we convened with the group for an entire day. I gave a presentation that described what we had heard—all those needs and desires and questions. The fourth generation decided to meet monthly to learn and discuss topics related to the family business, particularly focusing on relationships with wealth, career, and self-fulfillment. We let the group select the topics of the meetings and asked them to select a steering committee that would work closely with the consultants. Rachel and Ari volunteered, while Lia stepped back to let Ani take her place.

Fifteen next-generation members showed up to the monthly meetings to review and discuss issues pertaining to the business and their careers. They also explored their relationship with money: *What does it mean to have money? How do I handle my own budget? How do I choose among different things that I want to do or to own?* They talked about what ownership is, and where their careers were going. They also discussed some of the legal aspects of being owners of private companies, of publicly traded companies, and so on.

At the end of the first year, the steering committee raised the idea of sharing their experiences with their parents. They decided they would not make any requests or demands; they would simply say, "We just want to tell you about what we have done." The parents were totally surprised at what they heard. They said, "Next year, we want to be a part of this process too." After the steering committee presented a convincing budget that described the costs of a year's worth of personal and familial development, the parents even offered to pay for the process themselves.

The following year, the younger generation continued their monthly meetings, adding two yearly meetings with their parents. Together, both generations reviewed case studies of what other families had done to establish their governance and resolve dilemmas. Toward the third year the two generations decided to create three task forces: one that would be assigned to draft a Family Mission Statement, one that would create a program for next-gen education, and a third that would work on designing a Family Program (social events, a yearly retreat, a family forum, etc.).

The Grambar family process is now in its fifth year, and both generations continue to be involved. With the guidance of my colleague, Tal Yahav, the younger generation has established their own investment club, at the initiative of a few of the spouses. It has been their way of reinventing the business without burdening the senior generation with demands for change.

The effect has rippled upward. It has become obvious to everyone that the next generation was the catalyst for this process. As one senior member said, "It's a topsy-turvy world. Generation Four carries Generation Three on its shoulders."

What did the Grambar family learn from this process? The younger generation learned that in order to be a responsible owner, one has to be clear about one's values and relationship with wealth. As one of them put it, "I've decided that from now on, every decision I make will be based on my values." They realized that pursuing fulfilling careers might be more challenging for them than for educated young professionals from middle-class backgrounds and that sorting out their relationship with wealth would be necessary to ensure responsible financial behavior, constructive dialogue with their spouses, and the execution of their social responsibilities.

Another important takeaway came from the strength of the peer partnership. The group members now know one another's strengths and potential contributions. Newly able to work as a practiced team, they know how to assign tasks, manage disagreements, make decisions, communicate with the senior generation, and execute plans.

At the same time, they learned that not everyone can always participate in the group's activities. There are those who will join when it is right for them, even if they can't make it to every meeting. Still, the effect of having a working partnership amongst the next generation is significant, and makes the effort worthwhile, even with partial participation.

Finally, they learned that preparation for ownership takes time. The fourth generation of the Grambar family has worked for five years to prepare for succession, but they still feel that they have a way to go. They will continue to improve together, and as they keep moving, we are helping them pave their own road.

REINVENTION

How did you learn to walk? Was it by watching your parents walk around your nursery? Or was it by taking a step yourself, falling, and then trying again? Learning is not something we can rely on other people to do for us. If you want the next generation to know how to run the company, they must be allowed to learn the value of doing so themselves. They must feel that they have an impact on the company, so they'll understand the weight of their actions. This is why the next generation will need to reinvent processes and adjust expectations within the family business; as they do so, they'll be preparing themselves for ownership, management, decision-making, and most important, overcoming their mistakes.

Reinvention takes various forms. Within the enterprise, the younger generation may reinvent what the business does. They may change the product offering or start a new venture. Years ago, I went to a family business conference and spoke to a family that owned a chain of dry-cleaning shops all over England. One son was a computer science major, and his contribution to the business was to develop software for tagging laundry items with the customer's information. Eventually this software became a venture of its own, and the software was sold to other dry-cleaning chains all over Europe. By involving himself in the business, the son was able to help his family turn one business into two.

Reinvention may also focus on how the enterprise does what it does, particularly in the realms of new IT systems, online sales, or social media marketing. New management procedures, such as management meetings, written reports, or task forces, are all ways in which the business can be reinvented.

The role of ownership may also be reinvented by the younger generation, with the blessing and support of the senior one. John decided to focus on what the ownership did. When the family office sold its shares in the enterprise his grandfather had started, John led a campaign to have the proceeds reinvested in ventures that would have a positive social impact. John wanted to reinvent the core purpose of the business, going from a vehicle designed exclusively for wealth creation to one that would use that wealth to change the world for the better. In order to accomplish this, he had to educate all shareholders about socially responsible investments, investigate possible investments, and lobby both shareholders and family office professionals in support of those investments.

John is not alone in reinventing the meaning of ownership through giving. Most of the families I work with contribute to charities or are involved in some kind of philanthropy. It's usually the responsibility of one family member, often the head of the family or the head of the business, and he alone doles out significant sums to charity. Because this arrangement has been in place for so long, the rest of the family assumes that it should always be that way—until something changes and the next generation steps in and begins to ask questions like, "If we are allocating a significant amount of money to charity, what area of philanthropy interests each of us?" or "How do we make sure that the money we donate does what we want it to do?" or "What kind of control do we have?"

These types of questions push the family toward strategic philanthropy and away from simply donating to charity. The family's giving evolves into something that the individual members can do together, and it can even be assigned to someone who otherwise doesn't work in the business or is not interested in the day-to-day business activities. Going down this path ensures that the philanthropy is both effective and involves everyone. For someone who isn't involved in the business, taking charge of the family's philanthropic efforts can give their life a sense of meaning and purpose that they might otherwise have had a hard time finding. For the wealthy, philanthropy is not a luxury but a crucial tool for survival.

Younger people tend to be more interested in social responsibility and impact investing. The senior generation usually still sees a distinction between making money and donating it. But younger generations are less likely to separate the social and economic effects of doing business. The younger generation often looks for ways to bridge the gap between how money is made or invested and how money is donated. They reinvent ownership by being personally invested in the ideals of social responsibility and the greater good.

The fourth-generation Grambars opted not to interfere with financial decisions, but rather to establish a Family Council and Family Assembly. Their reinvention dealt with the *how* of ownership, rather than the *what*, by establishing new governance structures and introducing transparency into ownership matters—both of which are good examples of reinvention.

There are lots of ways to reinvent: In the business, one can change the *what* or the *how*—the product offering or the management procedures. Likewise, the ownership can affect *what* is done—new socially responsible investments, for example—or *how* ownership is governed. Each generation leaves its mark on the enterprise, and the cycle of maintenance to reinvention and back again is crucial to the health of the business.

CREATIVE SOLUTIONS

Within family businesses, the problems might be universal, but their solutions must be creatively tailor-made. I knew a young woman who liked inventing solutions. In trying to create a family agreement between herself and her siblings, she'd often run into strong pushback from one sibling in particular, which led to considerable familial conflict. Whenever her family began to feel desperate, however, she'd remind everyone that they could always find a solution. She could have taken a number of different approaches with her recalcitrant sibling, but she held onto her belief that the solution was a matter of invention, and this conviction has helped her guide her nascent family agreement through storm after storm.

Recently the association of small agricultural farms in Israel realized that because of the way the law is written,[3] only one successor can inherit a farm, which means that almost every family anticipates an eventual fight over succession. When I was approached to try to solve this problem, my response was, "Family businesses all solve their problems differently. I don't have an answer to this problem right now, but we can invent a solution." I suggested that we form a group of successors who would explore possible solutions and try to define a course of action.

---

3 Cooperative Associations Regulations, 1973.

When situations like this arise, my colleagues and I can lead families through a process that enables them to invent their own solution to their specific problem; there is no one-size-fits-all answer, no matter how much I'd like there to be.

CONCLUSION

I tend to place the responsibility for change on the next generation. I find that helping them become knowledgeable, aware, and competent is essential to the process of opening an effective dialogue with the parents or business owners. I know this seems counterintuitive, especially when all the resources, power, and authority are in the hands of the seniors, but I still encourage the younger generation to push forward with new ideas. Our evolving culture of innovation, collaboration, and community also helps to push this along.

Israel, like the rest of the world, moves fast, and the business world changes rapidly. A business needs the energetic pace of the younger generation if it is to grow and flourish. I once knew a founder who had been dominant in his family. He never let his son-in-law change anything in the business … until the day the son-in-law showed him that through the internet, he could reach a whole new pool of potential clients simply by "pressing one button on the computer." Since then, the son-in-law has had free rein to innovate.

Young people are the automatic heirs to every mistake the previous generation makes. They'll be the ones to pay the price for their elders' failure to deal with continuity issues. In a family business, there's no such thing as a win-lose situation; there is only win-win or lose-lose. If one family member "wins" and gains power over his siblings, he loses intimacy with his family, and his life becomes demonstrably worse—a lose-lose proposition. Successors, therefore, must have the greatest interest in setting things right and working together.

This process relies on effective checks and balances. Seniors bring to the table their wisdom, experience, relationships, and perspectives. The next generation brings innovation, entrepreneurship, familiarity with technology, a willingness to take risks, and an understanding of the current marketplace. Fusing these skills and strengths together into a strong family structure requires awareness and dialogue.

CHAPTER 5

It's All about Ownership

When God created the first human beings, God led them around all the trees of the Garden of Eden and said: "Look at My works! See how beautiful they are—how excellent! For your sake I created them all. See to it that you do not spoil and destroy My world; for if you do, there will be no one else to repair it."

Ecclesiastes Rabbah, 7

Smart families recognize that when it comes to maintaining the health and longevity of a family enterprise, the key issue is ownership. Questions dealing with central issues like who owns the business, how these persons came to own it, and what made them particularly suited to ownership can often influence the enterprise's strength and continued viability. The issues that emerge from these central questions are various: how decision-making takes place, what the best practices are for the enterprise's governance, and how the wealth is managed. Such issues will naturally dictate whether or not owners can affect the day-to-day business operations without interfering with the professionals' job. If addressed properly and if the right model is set up, these issues can help owners prepare their successors for responsible ownership.

Many of the patriarchs I meet have a **binary way of thinking** about their family business. They think in terms of two groups: family members involved in the business on one hand, and other family members on the other. For instance, patriarchs often tell me that one of their children works in the business and the others are "not involved at all." But when I ask them who they want to leave their wealth to, they inevitably say, "To all my children, equally." Simply put, they forget that wealth and the responsibilities of ownership are inextricably linked. I go on to ask if their equal distribution plan means that they intend to leave their contracting business (for example) to their daughter, whose medical practice is just beginning to take off, and to their son, who devoted himself to the cello at age ten and has shown no signs of pursuing anything else, in addition to the daughter who's been working for the business ever since she got her MBA. Once they start to think about the real-world ramifications of passing the weight of a fully operational business to a group of young people who are already busy forging their own separate paths, they begin to realize that the issue is more complex.

Ownership is not a meaningless title. Sometimes families focus entirely on the management of the business without considering what being an owner entails. When a patriarch declares that even though only one of his children works in the business he wants to leave it equally to all of them, he may not understand that doing so means they all will become owner-partners, even though only one of them has taken on the work of keeping the business going. This can be a recipe for conflicts, unless all the future owners take the time to learn what ownership and a working partnership mean.

The reality is that in any Family Business System, there are three groups, rather than two. "Owners" are their own distinct group, and that requires awareness and preparation.

THE DEFINITION OF OWNERSHIP

We usually define an owner as someone who legally possesses shares and therefore has the right to make decisions on behalf of a company. They receive a portion of that company's wealth and assets in compensation for those decisions. There *are* owners who aren't actually familiar with the responsibilities that go along with ownership, owners who are pursuing their own career while someone else—another family member, usually—makes most of the decisions that determine the future of the enterprise. But every owner should know that regardless of where they work in the business, or what career they pursue, they still have ownership responsibilities. In other words, someone may *knock on their door* if things go badly.

The Developmental Perspective

Understanding the relationship between family and ownership and the day-to-day workings of a family business is not intuitively simple, particularly for members of the founding generation. Founders are usually the family members, business managers, and owners. In other words, the three circles of the Venn diagram (see figure 3 below) are perfectly overlapping. At this phase, the founders don't need to think about the meaning of ownership. Their ownership has never been questioned. They also never need to stop and think, "Did I make the decision as owner, or as head of the family, or as CEO?"

But as time goes by, the three circles shift away from one another. For example, a spouse or a child can be a family member without working in the business and without being an owner. There may also be hired managers who are neither owners nor part of the family. There may also be strategic partners who *are* owners but are neither family nor participants in the business management. Each circle has a different population, and some people are in more than one circle. The roles of the people in these circles evolve as the circles expand and the people take on additional responsibilities.

Therefore, every generation after the founders, has to navigate a daily life in which they must comprehend the reality of the various positions and perspectives. As the relations between these three aspects of family business life (Family, Business, and Ownership) develop, generation after generation, responsibilities can overlap and boundaries need to be set. With time, the aspects (or circles, as they appear in the diagram) become ever more distinct.

The Family Business System

1. Family Members not involved in the business
2. Non-family/business owners
3. Non-family employees
4. Family owners not working in the business
5. Non-family owners who work in the business
6. Family members who work in the business but are not owners
7. Family owners who work in the business

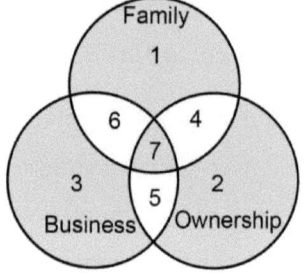

Figure 2. The Family Business System[4]

By placing themselves on the Venn diagram, family members can come to understand their roles and the conflicts they experience.

---

4 John A. Davis and Renato Tagiuri, "Bivalent Attributes of the Family Firm," *Family Business Review* (summer 1996).

It's worth paying attention to the perspectives and interests of each circle, because without an understanding of their unique needs and expectations, nearly any decision can create conflict. For example, if the board of directors (in the ownership circle) discusses the size of the dividend to be distributed to the owners, the family CEO (who is in all three circles) may want small dividends because he needs capital to buy new equipment for the business. However, his sister (who doesn't work in the business but is in the ownership and family circles) wants to buy an apartment, so she wants those dividends to be as large as possible. Conflicts that arise from such situations are common and are often interpreted as animosity among family members, instead of as the intermingling of different interests and points of view of well-meaning family members. The people who occupy different circles have different priorities. A better understanding of those priorities is the best way to defuse this kind of conflict.

There's an old joke about just this kind of role separation: A CEO called his marketing manager son into his office. "Joe, your performance has fallen short of our goals, and you've been underperforming for several quarters. I'm very sorry, but you're fired." The CEO escorts his ex-marketing manager out into the hall, where they both put on new hats. "Son," the father says, "I just heard you were fired. I'm so sorry. How can I help you?"

Keeping in mind the interplay between the circles of the Family Business System, I find myself focusing on the ownership circle, without being oblivious to the family concerns and business needs. I've found that ownership is the least understood circle. It's a fuzzy concept, but if you examine it from a variety of different angles, it builds a perspective that renders manageable most open issues and conflicts.

So, let's look at some aspects of ownership.

DUTIES AND PRIVILEGES OF OWNERS

The Strassberg family owns a large pharmaceutical enterprise. Leon, the grandfather, started the business in the early 1950s. He established strong contacts with major producers in Europe and held the license to import their products. His successors further developed the business, adding manufacturing pesticides, and real estate arms. In addition to the business's solid foundation, the founder left a heritage of extreme harmony among family members. When it came to continuing his legacy of industry and hard work, everyone was on the same page. The second-generation owners, a brother and sister, maintained a unique partnership. The two families spent a great deal of time together, including weekends and family vacations, among other events.

I met the family when the six cousins of the third generation were ready to start thinking about their careers and future ownership. As part of an education program designed to prepare them for ownership, we looked for a way to help them understand what ownership really means. I asked each of them to write down what they viewed as the duties and privileges of owners, in their specific family enterprise. We then collected their responses, and the following list was revealed (in no particular order).

DUTIES	PRIVILEGES
Professionalism/Quality	Money
Employees: protection, benefits, respect	Independence
Responsibility for the business's future	Reputation
Consideration of partners	Financial security

Partnership: coordination and synchronization	Employment
Respect for and acceptance of the external manager	Partners to share responsibilities with
Commitment to the business's values and heritage	Freedom to choose
Business proficiency	Influence
Knowledge of the industry sector and general business environment	
Familiarity with our business	
Proficiency in accounting	
Responsibility for the business's reputation	
Media handling	
Ethical behavior	
Backing, support, and control over CEO	
Setting vision and strategy	
Concern for environmental protection and sustainability	
Health and safety	

In the discussion that followed, the cousins were able to clarify for each other some of the less considered burdens and responsibilities of ownership. By thinking through some of the practical realities of ownership, they realized that they would have to acquire specific skills and areas of expertise to be ready for ownership, and once they understood what was entailed in running a business, new and even more specific questions arose. (Remember the importance of the *why* questions from chapter 3?) They decided to invite their parents to a meeting, to learn how they had handled certain issues and to further expand their concept of what their future as owners would look like. Eventually, this discussion resulted in the establishment of an individualized development program for each of them.

Setting the Rules of Engagement

Wearing several hats is complicated, and as subsequent generations come into their own, this situation becomes even more difficult. To avoid chaos, and to "protect the family from the business, and the business from the family," one needs to set clear rules.

Rules of engagement define who belongs where, who participates in what, and who is entitled to what. They are rarely defined in the first and second generation, but when they are, they become the cornerstone of the governance system. Establishing such rules can make the difference between continuity and selling the business. For instance, as long as the patriarch is around, people generally don't discuss his daughter's position and the salary she receives. But once he's not around, questions may arise: How should she be involved? What information should she receive? Who makes the decision regarding her salary? And so on. If the rules of engagement haven't been discussed, her occasional involvement will surprise and confuse everyone else. Without rules of engagement, no one will know how to resolve the conflict.

I once worked with a family of three second-generation owners who had decided that their spouses were not allowed to work in the business. A little while later, one of the owners married a man who also came from a family business, but in his organization, spouses were expected to take part. Moreover, his father was the son-in-law CEO of that family enterprise. Shortly after the honeymoon, the husband appeared in the office of his wife's family business and asked for a job and an office space. Her brothers looked at their sister: "Didn't we say no spouses?"

She just shrugged, "Yeah, but he really expects to be here."

In this case, the rules were set by the siblings in advance but were not communicated to the new brother-in-law. This incident caused a major crisis within the family. It's usually possible to head off this kind of conflict by setting the rules of engagement in advance, but if those rules are not communicated clearly to everyone involved, they cease to be effective. When these rules are written down and shared with anyone new to the family, many of the problems can be prevented.

Rules of engagement are particularly important when it comes to participation on the board of directors (the ownership circle). As long as the patriarch is in control, he decides who'll be on the board of directors. Everyone will accept his decision—or will very rarely express disagreement. But when the patriarch is gone, decisions about who sits on the board can spark a crisis. It is best to have the rules set clearly before any decision about a specific family member is made. Family members should be asking, "How should board members be selected?" rather than, "Why you and not me?"

Governing the Family Business System: Family Agreements

Rules of engagement are part of a larger set of family rules (a.k.a. Family Agreements, discussed in greater detail in chapters 9 and 10) designed to govern the interactions between family members and their assets. The larger a family is, and the more generations that are involved, the more important these rules become.

To create rules, owners must understand what exactly is at stake and be able to soberly discuss possible solutions. This process forces them to understand and internalize the deeper meaning of ownership, eventually allowing each of them to choose whether or not they want to continue being involved as owners. Documentation should only be completed and signed after the family has thoroughly discussed the issues and agreed upon the proposed solutions. Letting people really consider an issue and internalize the group's decision is the only way for such documentation to work. Without the willing participation of the family members, decisions enshrined in writing would not protect the family from fights when conflicts erupt.

It has been my experience that the written rules are important, but the memory of the discussions, the various opinions, and the agreement reached while making the rules are no less important. In addition, the Family Agreement serves as a document that shapes the expectations and plans of the younger generation. It communicates the family's values and vision for the future and solidifies their concept of the family business as a group venture—all of which will foster cooperation and collaboration while setting a model for long-term planning and conflict resolution within the family business.

Transferring Ownership: Discussing the Future Owner

Making clear decisions about ownership for the next generation, and ensuring that everyone is *aware* of the decision, enables potential successors to plan their own lives. If, for instance, one child wants to be a movie producer, she can move forward to pursue her dream career. If that child knows for certain that she will one day inherit her fair share (whatever "fair" means in her family), she won't base her career decisions on the fear of missing out. But if she doesn't know for certain, she might instead think, "Well, I want to be a movie producer, but maybe I should go to work in the store every day. I don't know if I'll get anything otherwise."

When family members who work in the business don't know how future ownership will be decided and when, they tend to think that continuing to work in the business entitles them to ownership or enables them to protect their interests. This is generally *not* true, but many people still act like it is. When someone doesn't know whether their position and interests are secure, their sense of powerlessness may soon translate into bitterness.

For example, a kibbutz close to Tel Aviv was operated on lands leased from the government in the 1940s, but for thirty years, the Knesset[5] hemmed and hawed over whether or not the members of the kibbutz would be allowed to assume ownership of the land they farmed. The kibbutz's proximity to Tel Aviv pushed up its property value, meaning that, if the Knesset decided that the kibbutz owned the land, the kibbutz members would be millionaires. An entire generation of kibbutz members—even the ones who weren't interested in farming—stayed on in the kibbutz in hopes that it would pay off. By the time the government decided to value all kibbutzim at 30 percent of their property values, the members were too old to start their lives over. They felt that they had wasted their lives hanging on to a false hope.

In addition, timing is key. There is the well-known joke about the senior who takes his 40-year-old son to the family plant and says, "One day, son, all this will be yours. But I am still waiting to receive it from my Dad." The consequences of this unfortunate situation are that the 40-year-old successor will continue to be "paper rich, cash poor" and feel powerless for an indefinite period of time. The senior, on his part, will continue to consider his successor "the child."

---

5   Israel's parliament.

I believe that:

1. Successors are not children. They reason like adults and have adult capabilities. They have to assume adult responsibilities.
2. There is nothing like being an owner, to practice ownership. Therefore, even if the senior keeps the majority of the shares in his control, transferring minority shares to the successors makes them feel like owners and behave like ones.

Nobody can force an owner to transfer all or some of his shares. But I usually recommend that seniors transfer a minority of their shares to their successors in order to create a true intergeneration partnership. This is the best way to practice ownership. Some seniors do it by announcing in advance when they will transfer shares. Others vow to do it as soon as they feel that the successors are "ready." While this is not a definitive timetable, I find that when a preparation process is in place, the promise is kept rather sooner than later.

Naturally, deciding on the future ownership and leadership also may involve choosing one offspring over others. The inability, or unwillingness of the seniors to choose the future leadership isn't just problematic when it comes to potential owners deciding how to build their lives. It can also affect one of the competitive advantages of family-owned enterprises (i.e., the ability to make decisions quickly by a small group of people).

The three Markston brothers were all over 70 years of age when I met them. They owned several real estate properties, which they managed themselves. The youngest of the three, Bill, was actively trying to sell the properties, as he had realized that they could no longer manage them well. But while he was trying to sell, Alan, the oldest brother, fell ill.

The Markstons all had big happy families, and Bill and his brothers realized that if something were to happen to one of them, there would be lots of inheritors, too many, who would have a hard time reaching an agreed-upon decision. If they took too long to make a decision about the properties, they might go down in value, and everyone would be impacted. To remedy the risk, they decided that one child in each branch should receive power of attorney to decide on behalf of their siblings. This decision was a step in the right direction, but each brother felt that he was unable to choose one of his children over the others. I took it upon myself.

I held a meeting with each group of siblings. In each meeting, we discussed the role of the person who would be appointed by the siblings: the demands of the position, including the substantial time requirement, and the qualifications and personality traits required of the right candidate. When we had a full "job description," I asked who, in their opinion, would be the most suitable to do the job. Each of the three groups reached a unanimous decision, without having to vote and without any bad feeling.

I could then return to the brothers and tell them that their children had successfully made their choice. At this point, all inheritors agreed to sign the power of attorney document, and the siblings secured the ability to make fast decisions, even if something were to happen to one of them.

Preparing Future Owners: The School of Ownership

While there are schools and courses focused on preparing students for careers in management, there are not too many programs that prepare them for ownership. Moreover, unlike what the founder sometimes tells himself, learning to be a responsible owner does not happen overnight. This process takes time. The sense of being responsible for everything that happens and doing it in partnership, is sometimes slow to develop. But when it kicks in, it usually inspires a strong desire to be there to represent the company and to lead the group during successes and failures.

The reality is that even if the founder was successful in creating and managing the business, he's not necessarily going to succeed at training his children to become efficient and engaged owners. No one learns to drive from watching their parent do it. To acquire ownership skills, successors need to be in the driver's seat, ideally with the patriarch sitting next to them, his hand on the emergency brake. Just watching will not cut it. This is why I urge families to look at succession as a three-phase process (see figure 3).

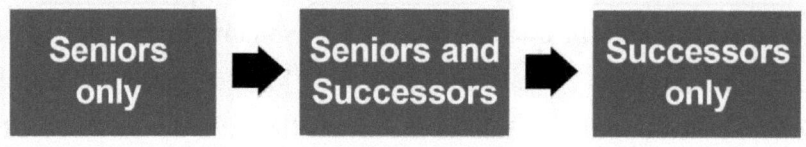

Figure 3. Three-phase process

If all goes well, the middle phase is long and allows plenty of opportunities to learn and develop. Simply mimicking the things you've seen the patriarch do will not be enough. To a certain extent, you'll need to reinvent the role to fit yourself. I once worked with a young man who would go around his company screaming at his employees. When I asked why he was screaming at people, he replied, "That's what Dad does." The man had not realized that his father personally knew every single employee and had developed relationships with them over the years. He knew their spouses, he'd given them loans when their luck ran low, and he'd made their lives better in dozens of other little ways. His son never saw any of that. He believed that he was fulfilling the role of owner by simply imitating his father.

Earning the trust and respect of employees is an additional challenge for the rising generation. Successors often say to me, "I don't have the respect of these people because they are loyal to my father." My advice is to approach the authority role slowly—to gradually gain respect while building your own team. Step by step, as it becomes possible, hire people who will be loyal to you.

CONCLUSION

Conscientious clients listen carefully to my lecture on the Family Business System and ask: "So what circle do you work for?" They're looking for evidence of hierarchy within the system, hoping for a judge to determine which circle of the Family-Business System overrules the others, and who within the system is unquestionably "in the right."

But true to my beliefs, I reply, "I work for the entire system." My duty is to make the three sub-systems work in collaboration, like cogs in a machine. When one changes, the others should always be affected.

Stewardship

It is impossible to end a discussion of ownership, without talking about stewardship. Healthy ownership is as much about having a long-term, responsible perspective as it is about humility. A new successor must say, *I'm not the creator of all this wealth and empire. I received ownership and I'm going to pass it on. I have to keep it working. I'm just one link in the chain.*

The Swiss master watchmaker, Patek Philipe, ran an ad some years ago that has always stuck with me—a photo of a handsome man's watch above the following text: "You never really own a Patek Philipe. You just keep it in good shape for the next generation." While one hesitates to accept aphorisms from magazine advertisements, the truth is that this statement reveals the essence of stewardship.

When preparing next-generation clients for ownership, the work I do is based on the assumption that when owners experience their ownership as more than a transaction, they act in committed ways that translate into active stewardship of the entire enterprise. In turn, good stewards care for their assets by investing in them to the benefit of their family, associates, and the broader community.

Effective stewards understand what "built to last" means and recognize that while financial value is important, it is only one aspect of the foundation of their family's enterprise. They appreciate that legacy is composed not just of material goods, but also of deeply held values. They realize that when material wealth is stripped of the values that led to its creation, the whole family is in peril.

As a member of the Jewish people, I feel that I am a link in a long chain that stretches back three thousand years. I didn't start the chain nor will it end in my lifetime. Awareness of this continuity fosters a necessary sense of humility. The business and family that you may belong to are very powerful, and the danger is that this dynasty could open the door to a sense of entitlement. Instead of feeling entitled, you should cultivate a sense of obligation to do right by all stakeholders: family, employees, customers, suppliers, regulators, and the community. This is the responsibility that comes with stewardship. This is the meaning of ownership.

CHAPTER 6

The Unspoken Evils of Wealth

The more possessions, the more worry.

Ethics of the Fathers (Pirkei Avot), 2;7

Sometimes on the weekend, my husband and I take a walk out to the little café down the street. We sit on the patio and drink coffee as the afternoon wears on, and we watch as people pass, absorbed in their lives. One such afternoon, we came across a young family, also seated on the patio. The mother had a sheaf of papers she was frantically poring over—no doubt preparing for the following day, even in this tranquil setting—while the father discussed the coming week's agenda with their daughter, who couldn't have been older than eleven. Together they listed event after event: lacrosse practice, a violin recital, a Tae Kwon Do lesson, tutoring, and several upcoming tests in school for which the child needed to study.

I listened as, in each case, the father recounted the benefits of each of these pursuits: how they all wove together to support his daughter's growing brain and body, and how they all contributed to her eventual mastery of skills—which the father admitted to not having attained himself. I'm no stranger to the concept of "helicopter parenting," but this didn't seem to be that. He wasn't trying to protect his daughter from life. Rather, it seemed like he and his wife had seen a certain amount of social and financial success that they hadn't been born into. They had climbed several rungs up the ladder, and it looked like they wanted to help their child continue that ascension.

Wealth and success aren't just a means for attaining comfort and power. They also create opportunities, and in those opportunities, people tend to look for things they can do to improve the lives of their family members. There's nothing wrong with that. The impulse to make your child's life better than your own is one of the classic driving purposes behind most wealth accumulation. However, the reality of trying to improve your child's life can have undesired consequences. I still remember watching that little girl's face as her entire week unfolded and seeing her expression droop when she realized there was no time left for her to play with her friends. Her parents were giving her *so* much that she was losing her grip on the things that were uniquely her own.

This problem isn't limited to any single culture. I recently gave a lecture to a group of Chinese families regarding lesser-known aspects of Israeli heritage and family life, and in the questions that followed, I noticed a similar phenomenon. The teenage listeners all felt that the hopes and aspirations their parents had *for them* were preventing them from playing, relaxing, or exploring their own aspirations. While these kids were good kids—kids who genuinely wanted to honor their parents—it was clear that they felt smothered.

All parents who own wealth want that affluence to enhance the development of their children (or siblings, or cousins, depending on the family structure). Everyone wants the wealth to help individual prospects to improve, and everyone wants the relationships among their family members to grow in trust and warmth. I've asked every senior I've come across, and no one has disputed this idea. But the truth is that, regardless of how benevolent our hopes are, wealth doesn't actually work this way. Often, wealth has the opposite effect.

METEORIC DISRUPTION

In *The Cycle of the Gift: Family Wealth and Wisdom*, authors James E. Hughes Jr., Susan E. Massenzio, and Keith Whitaker put forward the somewhat novel idea that people need to be prepared for wealth before they receive it. When significant wealth is given to young people who have not been sufficiently prepared, that wealth can crush them, much like a meteor flying out of nowhere to crash into a young person's plans and disrupt every part of the life they created.

Most people's lives are spent in "survival mode" (whether we acknowledge it or not), a perspective that seeks accomplishment for the sake of *survival* over any other motive. From this perspective, a job is important because it lets you pay rent. It lets you put food on the table. It lets you take care of your children. The question of *why* isn't really important because survival is the obvious, undisputed answer. But once you get beyond survival—once you've accrued enough wealth to make rent a nonissue, to afford enough food to keep your family and yourself fed for the foreseeable future—that's when the *why* question becomes more important. That's when you start thinking seriously about meaning and how you can find value in your own life. And it's a challenge. We all face it on our own. Your parents can't really help you. And, more confusingly, it's a challenge that affluence—by definition—cannot overcome.

For most every other problem that affluent families have faced, money has been instrumental in the solution to the problem. The discovery that developing a sense of personal value and meaning cannot be aided by money flies against experience and history, but it is nonetheless true. The confusion and anxiety that result from that discovery are part of what the aforementioned authors mean when they talk about the meteorically disruptive properties of a poorly timed gift of wealth.

Finding Meaning and Self-Fulfillment

It's hard to recognize that you or your child may be unprepared for wealth. It took several expert lectures and discussions among members of her Gen Peer group for a fourth-generation successor to come to that conclusion—to understand that finding self-fulfillment was going to be much more difficult for her than for people who worked in order to pay rent at the end of the month. She realized that she would have to work much harder to create a significant and fulfilling career for herself.

A third-generation member, along with some cousins, spent time exploring the legacy of their family's founders and their own values. This man had chosen to study medicine and wanted to devote his life to saving lives and helping people. He realized that he would not earn nearly as much as his cousins who would be in the family business, but he felt that the family's wealth made it possible for him to make this professional choice. As it does for everyone, it took time and work for the man to realize that when wealth comes into play, money ceases to serve as a yardstick for decision making. It's no longer the case that your options are limited by what you can afford. You have to find another means of deciding between one course of action and another. At this point, values are the only valid compass for one's behavior.

LOVE AND MONEY: THE GIVING PLAN

Beyond personal motivations, carelessly given wealth can wreak havoc on family relationships. Successors tend to think of inheritance as love translated into money, which can have hurtful results on either side of the generational divide. If one successor receives more than their siblings, it may be interpreted as if the parent loved them more, sparking jealousy, accusations, and feelings of inferiority—all of which erode family relations. The successors aren't usually jealous of the money itself, but the implication that one successor's relationship with the parent is somehow more valuable than that of another successor can be heartbreaking. Even among very affluent siblings, the idea that the parent loved another sibling more is unacceptable. It may cause fights. It is difficult to be a parent in this sort of situation, simply because no matter how dedicated the parent is, it's very hard to give an exactly equal gift. The dilemma of basing the giving on equality or on fairness is a problem that every parent has to face. Fairness is deeply subjective, so it must be carefully communicated. The alchemy involved here is complex.

Individual responses to suddenly receiving wealth are not as straightforward as a simple financial transaction. In each circumstance, the expectations on both sides of the equation must be taken into account. The giver's motives—conscious or not—may color how the receiver understands the purpose of the gift, while the needs of the receiver—known and unknown—may end up coloring the giver's motives or may alter the receiver's sense of obligation. On top of that, the circumstances surrounding the gift (what we call the gift's "habitat") can also affect every other moving part of this transaction. When giving, it is essential to consider the motives, feelings, and habitat that accompany the gift of wealth.

Hughes et al. go into this subject in more depth, exploring the complexity of giving and the factors that should be considered. They also provide several lovely ideas for getting it right. They pose a basic question: "How can one give wisely to one's family members so that it promotes their growth, independence, and prosperity?" Their answer is that the giver should know themselves and their motivations, as well as those of the receiver.[6]

I love *The Cycle of the Gift*. Hughes et al. have beautifully described the very dilemmas I've spent so much time trying to communicate to my clients. I felt so strongly about this book that when I headed the Family Advisory Services of UBS in Israel, I suggested we have the book translated into Hebrew and given as a gift to our clients. It was exciting to see how each of our clients found a different thought, story, or explanation that made them rethink their attitude toward giving.

BE NICE

My colleague, Menahem Yablonski, at Dorot, developed the NICE™ model (see figure 4), based on some of the ideas presented in *The Cycle of the Gift*. He wanted to illustrate the complexity inherent in the process of giving.

Givers and receivers may have different motivations regarding the transfer of wealth. These differences are often at the root of misunderstandings, ingratitude, and even a number of conflicts.

---

6   James E. Hughes Jr., Susan E. Massenzio, and Keith Whitaker, *The Cycle of the Gift: Family Wealth and Wisdom* (Princeton, NJ: Bloomberg Press, 2012).

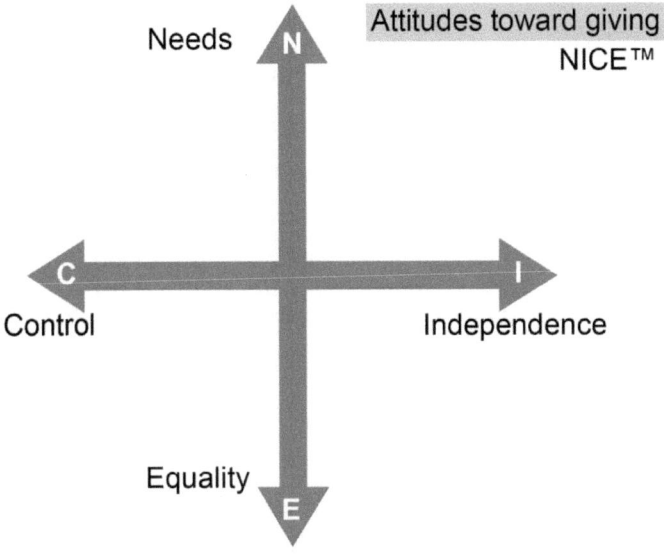

Figure 4. NICE™ model: Attitudes toward giving

This model illustrates the ways in which the motivations of the giver may be in conflict with those of the receiver. For instance, a parent may want to give wealth so as to maintain control over some aspect of the receiver's life, which is directly at odds with the receiver's need for independence. The parent might also give specifically to encourage their child's independence, knowing that they'll have to relinquish some control to achieve that goal. On the other axis, they might believe in giving equally to all their children, which may mean that some—with potentially greater needs than others—end up feeling shortchanged by the process. By the same token, if they give according to need, the inequality may also lead to resentment.

The unspoken differences in attitude around the giving of wealth can easily cause tension between family members. I worked with one set of successors who proposed a giving model in which the parents gave an equal amount to each child, while each child managed their own expenses. The parents liked the plan, but they had one problem: the mother wanted the freedom to pay for her grandchild's nanny, rather than have his parents put him in day care. Her words were, "What good is my money, if I cannot even save my grandchild from being put in day care too early?" This went entirely against the ethos of the plan, but to the mother, it seemed perfectly reasonable. Her unspoken attitude—that her money could control her children's parenting choices—wound up sinking the whole project. They could not come to an agreement.

Similarly, after the parents of another set of successors agreed to give an equal amount to each child so they could buy their own homes, one son came to them, asking for a loan. He wanted to buy a house that cost more than the amount they'd given to their other children. His unspoken attitude—that his needs and wants entitled him to more money than his siblings—was in direct conflict with the rest of his family.

On the flip side, I also worked with a family in which the parents simply bought their son a house. However, the ongoing maintenance of the house—utilities, taxes, a gardener, cleaning staff, etc.—ended up being more than their son could afford on his family company's salary. This created a permanent dependence on his parents' help. I've found that asking parents and children to place themselves on the NICE model can help them understand the conflicts that are tearing apart their relationships.

Differences between Mom and Dad on the NICE™ Model

There are a lot of ways in which giving is a complicated process, and the NICE™ model can only go so far. It doesn't, for instance, show the additional complexity that arises from the different giving styles of two individual parents. I have often discovered that procrastination or mistakes in the giving result from differences of underlying assumptions between the parents.

When I work with parents on a giving plan, I begin with a set of questions exploring their childhood memories: the financial realities of their childhood, their parents' attitudes toward money, how they went about asking for money from their parents, and their first experiences with earning money. I interview each parent separately, letting the other be a quiet listener. Couples who have been together for most of their adult lives are amazed at how their different childhood situations affect their current attitudes toward money.

Diane and Bob came to me when they started planning the way they wanted to give to their children. The idea was to decide in advance what, when, and how each child would receive wealth over the course of the parents' lives, and how the remainder of that wealth would be distributed after the couple was gone. Diane and Bob were in their early sixties. Both were engineers, the owners of a successful engineering firm. They had four children. In pulling from their engineering background, they knew that they wanted to have their plan laid out in advance so they could follow it to the letter. But when they listened to each other's childhood stories, they immediately realized that they needed to spend more time thinking about this process.

Diane trusted that "everything would be OK," because she came from a well-to-do family. Her parents had always been there to help when needed. Bob, on the other hand, was a self-made man who'd grown up in a modest home. He was always concerned that "there would not be enough." Bob's parents had distributed the little they had unevenly among their children. They had discussed it openly with their children before their deaths, explaining that one child needed more help than the others. Bob had no problem with the needs-based method of giving. Diane's parents, however, had always been careful to give equally, and Diane couldn't see the value of any other way of doing things. It was only when Diane and Bob saw and understood the source of their differences that they could discuss them openly, without getting emotional. They soon came up with a plan that fit their own family situation.

Money and power are often tied together. That is especially true when parents feel insecure about their relationships with their children. An attempt to "secure" contacts and relationships through financial dependence is very tempting. Many parents do it—some knowingly, some not. One patriarch told me outright that he wanted to follow this strategy, saying, "I was absent during most of their childhood, and now they side with their mom. If they don't need my money, they may not come see me at all." It sounds terrible, but I was glad, at least, he was honest about his motivation.

THE CHALLENGES AROUND WEALTH AND GIVING

When it comes to the "habitat" of the gift, there are some additional challenges to be tackled: namely, the reactions from friends and society at large.

Jealousy

People giving and receiving wealth are often on the hard end of jealousy, and they can find themselves tangled up in friendships that are guided more by money than genuine human companionship. This can result in shame, guilt, and a whole host of suspicion-related side effects. To combat this eventuality, young people from affluent families often hide their family identity, afraid that it will interfere with the authentic relationships they want to have with others. I once knew a girl from a very rich family, who was serving in the military alongside a boy from another rich family. "I know that he is from the *X* family," she told me, "because of his last name, but he does not know that I am from the *Y* family." Her hidden identity gave her confidence in her relationship with this boy. Hiding one's identity cannot be long lasting. But in some cases, it buys precious time. It allows youngsters to establish their own identity, find meaningful careers, and feel better prepared to handle jealousy.

Entitlement

Most of the parents I meet are deeply concerned that their children, in response to wealth, will develop a sense of entitlement. It frightens them! If the parents are first-generation founders, they are usually outright appalled at the thought that their children might someday feel entitled. But even when the parents are second- or third-generation successors, they still want to avoid that possibility. Fortunately, in all my years of work with families, I have come across very few successors who felt entitled.

I say "very few" because I did encounter some of these individuals, and they were very unpleasant to work with. I would describe working with these successors as being a demanding process. Not that there's anything wrong with demanding excellence, or precision, or quality; but in the case of working with these young people, I found that their demands came from the perception that they had power, and they simply felt like flexing it. They acted from extreme selfishness. But more than that, when I set aside the unpleasant working atmosphere, I found myself mostly concerned about their mental strength—their ability to stand on their own feet and fend for themselves. If all their lives they had felt that they didn't need to take action to achieve their goals, but could instead simply demand results from others, it seemed to me that they lacked a backup plan. If anything ever went wrong, their first strategy would be to look for someone else to fix it, rather than taking positive steps on their own.

For instance, when I worked with a group of siblings from a very wealthy family, we got into a conversation about the role of the consultant. I told them that I considered myself their guide on the journey they were taking. As their guide, I could show them the way, I could recommend suitable gear, I could warn them about an upcoming river or cliff, and I could plan the length of the trip with them. But eventually, they would have to reach the top of the mountain on their own two feet. Sharon, the youngest of the siblings, listened carefully, and then commented, "We could also get to the top of the mountain by helicopter."

Entitlement doesn't happen in a vacuum. The parent-child relationships that may create this kind of toxic attitude often stem from the most innocent of motivations—the desire to protect your child from pain—that every parent experiences. But no matter how much a parent wants to do that, we all know that at some point, our power as a parent will reach its limit, and our children will have to set off into the world to forge their own paths. And that's a good thing. But what happens if a parent never reaches that limit? If a parent can truly protect their child from hardship? For lots of wealthy parents, particularly those who've had to struggle to create their wealth, the temptation to shield their child from pain and disappointment is too strong to resist. The result is an entitled child. And while entitled offspring are difficult to work with, the destructive side effects of this kind of sheltering aren't limited to awkward social encounters. This kind of relationship is primarily destructive to the parent-child relationship itself. For many of these cases, and as a result of such protection, even when the successors reach their thirties and forties, their parents love them but do not necessarily admire them. I have seen heads of enterprises who love their children and speak often about their "potential," but that doesn't mean they're going to promote them. These leaders have respect and admiration for the managers that work for them, the ones who struggled and kept working to achieve the goals they set for themselves. For many leaders, the character that comes from overcoming hardship is a prerequisite to trust and admiration, and without that character, the children of the leader will not enjoy the parental respect they seek.

Anne was a case in point. She was the daughter of a very successful entrepreneur who demanded a lot from the managers who worked for him. His daughter was well-educated and potentially capable, but her career struggled to get off the ground. I first met her when she was in her early fifties, still waiting for her father's recognition, feeling frustrated every time that respect and recognition did not arrive. It wasn't that he didn't love her. He certainly did. But he did not admire her the way he admired his colleagues and trusted employees.

Damaged Career Ladders

Career paths are much like ladders. You start at the bottom, earn experience through more or less gratifying jobs, and gradually acquire the knowledge and skills required to move up the ladder. In the process, you also develop the ability to endure long hours and physical hardships, to work for less-than-perfect bosses, to manage tricky work environments, and generally grow into a person who can get things done regardless of the circumstances.

But for the young people who come from wealthy families, this traditional ladder is often missing a rung. Out of a sincere intention to protect them, their parents may say something like, "You don't need to stay in that job if the hours are too long, or if the boss is too demanding. You/we have enough money to support you." The young person follows the parents' suggestion and quits. And then, because they have no experience sticking out an uncomfortable situation, it happens again. And again. Until they find themselves at the age of thirty-five with a stalled career and no stable path or track record. This is when this person may look around and see their colleagues advancing up the career ladder, while they are still looking for the perfect opportunity.

Parents invariably tell me that their son or daughter has great potential. When I ask how old their child is, and I learn that they are forty or forty-five, I have to explain to the parent that "potential" is a term that has a limited shelf life. You can talk about the "potential" of someone who's twenty-three, but by the time that kid hits forty-five, you should really be talking about "track record." Parents often don't see the way their wealth has had a negative effect on the development of their children.

INTERNAL ARMOR

How can we guard against the negatives of wealth? There is no one magic remedy, but there is an internal armor we can cultivate to cope with the negative effects of wealth. These are relevant for both the parents and the successors.

Parental awareness. Think deeply about your own motives and those of others. Why, specifically, do you want to give *this* person *this* amount of money? What do you hope that doing so will achieve?

Giver's honesty. Be open about the extent to which you want to control others with money. Hughes et al. discuss this in greater detail.

A few years ago, we worked with a family on their constitution. When the parents met with me to discuss how they wanted to give to their children, I learned that they wanted to give equally, except in the case of their gay son. The mother wanted to give him more "in order to help him." She apparently was unaware of her own attitude toward his sexual orientation and genuinely wanted to help him. When we confronted her with her motives, she changed her mind.

Values and motives. Make a point of exploring your family values and analyze them. Explore their location on the NICE™ model. Make sure that your values and vision become the true yardstick for your decisions and your behaviors.

Develop a sense of cause and self-fulfillment. When children grow up, they tend to excuse the ways their parents have let them down—things like being at work when they came home from school, missing a birthday, etc. They do not excuse, however, a parent who has led an unfulfilled life. Having an unfulfilled parent as a role model inevitably affects a person's life for the worse. Those children will eventually have to invent their own way of finding purpose while fighting against the unfortunate parental model.

Turn your situation to your advantage. Money gives you options. It can let you pursue a cause, regardless of whether it will benefit you financially. I worked with an affluent family in which two of the siblings entered the family business, while the third—a woman—went to medical school. Together they realized that, because she had the financial backing of her family, she could afford to study for many years, putting years of work into the hospital and dedicating her life to the betterment of human health. They decided that she would be granted a certain standard of living that would enable her to pursue her cause. For them, this arrangement was an honorable way of using family wealth.

Social responsibility. Engage your family in socially responsible activities. Transition from charity to strategic philanthropy and social responsibility. This should be something the family identifies and does together. Most of the younger generation family members are very interested in this area. Rebecca, for instance, a young client, used philanthropy as a means of developing meaning, leadership, professionalism, and self-esteem, together with her connection to the family legacy. When Rebecca reached the middle of her life and her children had already left home, she realized that her life so far had been dedicated to keeping the family together. She had spent every day working for the common good of the family, and she felt like she'd missed out on a crucial opportunity for self-esteem and fulfillment. To remedy this problem, she decided to sell her shares in the family enterprise and use her wealth for large-scale philanthropic projects. She announced to her family that this would be her project, rather than a family endeavor. Over the years, she developed her activity into a high-level, professionally operated social endeavor. She became an inspiring leader in the field and a model for her family and for many philanthropists around the world.

Sense of belonging. By anchoring yourself and your family to a larger community and using that anchor point to pursue your passions, you can find a larger sense of identity that relies on yourself and your family, separate from affluence. For example, my client, Galit, is a third-generation member of a family that owns art galleries and auction houses. When she and her family wrote their Family Agreement, they specified:

> *We are a warm and loving family who identifies itself with the world of art. We have been historically connected with art for three generations. We love art and live it through a daily connection between family and work. We aspire to continue this connection into the future. At the same time, we aspire to do good, both as a family and an enterprise.*

The family decided to dedicate part of its activities to philanthropy by allocating spaces for artists, holding free art classes for children with special needs, and contributing a sum of money for the promotion of artistic activities throughout the country. For Galit, a connection to the art world is part of her identity. By linking her desire to "do good" with the family business, she was able to build up her sense of belonging and self-fulfillment.

CONCLUSION

The evils of wealth are neither a necessity nor a destiny. They can be overcome. It takes awareness, integrity, hard work, planning, and investment. As Rebecca used to say, "We invest in peace. War is much more expensive, and we do not want to waste our money on war."

All the examples I presented in this chapter are taken from affluent families, but not from the richest of the rich. It's easy to dismiss the movie *Born Rich* by saying, "We are not as rich as they are. This does not affect me." But the truth is that I have deliberately discussed negatives to which every family with some wealth might be exposed. Recognizing the risks can be the beginning of reversing the predictable negative outcomes.

It is possible for family members to use wealth to enhance the development of their loved ones and bring the family closer together. I know numerous families who have achieved this feat.

CHAPTER 7

What Do Parents Really Owe Their Children?

A Parent is obligated to teach their child a vocation. Rabbi Yehuda says: 'Whomever does not prepare their child with a vocation, it is as if they have taught them thievery.'

Talmud, Kiddushin, 29

This book has been written with the successors in mind. This particular chapter is intended to be shared with the seniors. I would hope that it can open a constructive dialogue between seniors and successors. After all, such dialogue is one of the most important keys to a successful continuity.

Some years ago, I met Dina, who arrived at my office with her oldest son (who was twenty-nine at the time). Dina was in her late fifties, and she was the sole owner of a medium-sized family business that was doing pretty well. She told me that the business had been founded by her late husband Simon, a great entrepreneur and a relentless worker. Simon died suddenly about ten years after the business was founded, leaving Dina with five young children.

At the time of the accident Dina had been a social worker. Although she did not know much about the business, she had decided it must continue. A trusted employee was managing the operation, so she let him stay and appointed him CEO. He did a good job, and after a year he came to her asking for shares of the business, in recognition of his excellent performance and his loyalty in this time of crisis.

Dina was quick to acknowledge his contribution, but regarding the shares, her first instinct was to tell him, "I cannot give you what is not mine. This business belongs to my children, and I am keeping it for them. I cannot give you what is theirs." As owner and mother, she felt that she owed it to her children to keep their father's business running so that eventually, when they were ready for it, they could take over.

The years were kind, and Dina made a number of other wise decisions, managing to keep the business thriving and profitable. Two of her children have since joined the business. Another two are involved and are active future owners.

Dina's response to her trusted employee was instinctive, intuitively grasping her obligations to her children. But not every parent has that bone-deep certainty. For many parents, finding the right answer is difficult and a cause for many sleepless nights.

A little while ago, I hosted a very small dinner party—just me, my husband, and another couple, Leah and Eitan, whose children had grown up with ours. We'd known them for more than twenty years, and between us we'd shared countless struggles and triumphs. That night, as the twilight faded and bits of dessert were left at the table, we were sitting out on the back deck, discussing their son Ariel's surprising decision to move to Australia. Eitan set down his wine glass with a finality that heralded a question he'd clearly been pondering for some time. "What do I really owe my children?" he asked.

This isn't an unusual question, though we don't hear it very often. Personally, I think that most parents ask it of themselves late at night, or in very private circles. Asking it in public feels unkind, or perhaps just unseemly. In public, parents will say things like, "I worked so hard. I did it all for you. I wanted you to be secure and protected, and that's why I worked so hard." But the follow-up to that sentence—*very* rarely heard in public—usually goes in one of two directions.

The first continues with, "And therefore, I don't owe you anything else. I provided very well for you. I guess you'll do whatever you decide to do, but if you ruin it all, it's your problem." As a passive-aggressive statement of disengagement, this acknowledges the child's autonomy without respecting it. It builds more barriers than it takes down.

The second is no less destructive: "And therefore, the least you could do to pay me back is stay here and preserve what I've built, whether you like it or not." This second version was Eitan's meaning. He'd spent his life building a successful law firm, and Ariel's decision felt like a slap in the face—a repudiation of everything he'd worked so hard for.

But the truth is that Eitan's life's work was never about his concern for his son. Certainly, he'd wanted to ensure that Ariel and his sister were secure and protected, but all the work he'd done *after* that goal was achieved was work that he'd *wanted* to do. Founders and seniors aren't driven exclusively by their concern for the next generation. No one is. People—founders especially—are driven by passion, talent, and the tremendous personal satisfaction they derive from success. They don't do it for their children solely; they do it for themselves.

And that's perfectly all right, as long as they acknowledge that fact. Acknowledging it relieves the next generation of the sense that they are in debt to their parents. It lets them shed any guilt they might feel for choosing a career outside the family business. Eitan had spent his life building a successful firm, and Eitan's son had decided to start a winery in Australia. Neither of these facts should be interpreted as being aimed at the other.

Apart from advocating for a general sense of self-awareness, I'm not trying to change the senior generations. I don't know what "perfect parents" look like. I've not yet met one. There is no "perfect parent" mold for me to stuff anyone into. Rather, this chapter is devoted to the parents whose sons or daughters *do* want to continue the enterprise, the wealth management, or the family legacy. What do parents really owe them? What are the obligations a parent should attempt to keep as their part of the deal of continuity?

Over the years, I've worked with hundreds of families, and in 2016, we conducted an extensive survey regarding the success factors that contribute to bringing a successor fully into the family business.[7] I've learned that there are specific behaviors parents can use to build

---

[7] In 2016, I along with my colleague, Ms. Tal Yahav, conducted a program for a major bank in Israel. Over several months, we met with 160 owners and successors of family-owned businesses. They participated in the program in pairs, so that we had a senior and a junior from each family. Part of the program consisted of separate facilitated group discussions for both the seniors and the juniors. In each group, the topic for discussion was "What are the key success factors that contribute to a successful integration of the next generation in the family business?" The discussions in the groups were very lively. People were happy to share their experiences, dilemmas, and disappointments with their equals. Some of the insights and recommendations we collected have been incorporated into this chapter. It is rare to have such a large sample of family business owners. The data in this chapter is unique in that it comes from the owners and the generation that will follow them. I want to thank the participants in these groups for sharing their experiences and their wisdom, as well as the Leumi Bank, for sponsoring the program.

their relationships with their successors and ease their own minds regarding what, specifically, they owe them. This chapter is based on the study we conducted, as well as on my many conversations with those family members.

PREPARING THE NEXT GENERATION

Scripture tells us that every parent owes their child training in a vocation, lest without it, that child turns to harmful behavior for the sake of survival. In the case of a family enterprise, the "vocation" is the ownership. Therefore, seniors owe their children preparation to become future owners. This includes financial and business skills, naturally, but also training in partnership, the ability to speak productively with the senior generation, social responsibility, and stewardship. Seniors sometimes feel uncomfortable opening up sensitive issues. They may argue that they have given their children the wealth or the enterprise, and what happens after their death is none of their concern. I often answer them with the quote that opened this chapter.

Modeling Partnership

Not everyone is set up to prepare their successors in all of the skills that would make them effective owners. It's worth remembering that most founders are lone creators. They don't always know how to be partners, let alone teach partnership. Some of them don't even believe in partnerships. As one founder put it, "If God thought that partnership was a good idea, He would have a partner." As fond as he was of this little saying, it didn't stop him from wanting a harmonious partnership among his children. But even if the senior generation cannot provide a partnership model, simply acknowledging that partnership is a complex arrangement can spur further action. It's essential to understand that in a partnership, leadership is characterized by acting in a collaborative manner, rather than an authoritative one. If the senior has the awareness to realize they cannot provide a model of participative leadership, they should support the successor's attempts to develop it on their own.

Choosing the Leader of the Next Generation

Parents don't want to discriminate among their children. They want to maintain the perception that they have no favorites and love everyone equally. While that may well be true, by neglecting to choose a successor, they may create a lifetime of strife and infighting for their children. Natural sibling rivalries, jealousy, and competition will feed the battle for years to come—a battle that will only grow worse as the family grows and spouses come into play.

My client, Martin, was the second-generation leader of a medium-sized consumer product company. He received a small and struggling company from his parents and turned it into a well-established, innovative enterprise. He was entrepreneurial and always viewed his company as "big," even when that wasn't technically the case. He appointed high-level experts from overseas as external directors of his board of directors and hired a professional CEO even though he was still perfectly capable of running the business himself. "This way I can be full-time chairman," he explained. "The company needs that."

Martin has three children, and his brother/partner has three of his own. Very early on, when his oldest son was about fifteen, Martin started to groom him for the leadership position. He took the son with him to receptions and on trips and told him that he would one day take over. The son was prepared "by the book," receiving a college degree, management experience outside of the family business, and gradual advancement up the company ladder, as well as help from the best consultants and the constant support of his father. Martin's second son, a dynamic and perfectly capable young person, never had a chance at similar attention and resented it.

Martin knew that he wasn't treating his sons equally, but he said, "I shall invest whatever I need to in order to make sure the relationship between my sons is healthy, but I'm not going to sacrifice the interests of my business for it." True to his word, he hired a top consultant to work with his family, establishing governance structures and ensuring open communication among everyone. The second son was eventually granted individual coaching and career support, as needed. It took several years, but eventually he was able to say, "I am grateful to my father for standing firm, and to my brother, for carrying the heavy burden of everyday leadership. I earned my freedom, and I am the best partner to my brother that I can possibly be." Since the older brother took over, the business quadrupled in size and became a global conglomerate.

The founders of the Weinberger family business took a less firm approach to succession planning. The parents had founded a printing business, and it was doing well when their daughter and two sons came to work with them. Each child had their own strength and was assigned a distinct role in the business. The parents wanted to believe that because their children's capabilities seemed so different, they would naturally fall into a harmonious working relationship, saving the parents the painful duty of choosing one of them to be "first among equals."

I met the siblings thirty years after their parents' deaths, when they were close to retirement themselves. The third generation had brought me in, explaining that fighting among the siblings was taking the business down. I made an attempt to restore peace and collaboration, but it was obviously too late. They admitted that having never confronted the issue of who should lead was a grave mistake that had cost the business its success.

Powers of the Successor

Parents should be sure to give the chosen successor responsibility over the business and/or finances, but *not* any responsibility that can be construed as "parental" over their siblings. I had one client whose chosen son entered the family business and initiated a "survey" of his brothers' and sisters' financial situations, vis-à-vis the family office, ostensibly as data collection for his father, who wanted to plan his giving. This gave him access to information detailing how much each of them earned and what they spent—in other words, information people don't show to their close friends, let alone the kid they still maybe resent for that time he put a frog in their bed. I told the son to back away from the project, which was leading him to step into the role of "father" rather than business leader.

Parents can easily confuse their actions as business and financial leaders with their roles as parents, so to be very clear: the son *cannot* be the "father" of his siblings. They do not want him to have that authority. They do not want to be dependent on him (or even more upsetting, *indebted* to him) for the rest of their lives. Throughout their childhoods, he has been their equal, their peer. They're going to have a hard time letting go of that mind-set.

Financially Supporting a Preparation Program

At Dorot, we help next-generation leaders prepare themselves for leadership positions in the family business. Working with the successor and their family, we build roadmaps for professional and personal development, and we map out any specific course work and preparation they should have. We also establish mechanisms for follow-up and the eventual evaluation of their progress.

Our client, Sam, was thirty-one years old when we met him. His parents Marvin and Michelle founded their consumer products manufacturing business when they were a young couple. The business grew slowly, and for many years it struggled to survive. It was only in the last few years that they felt like they were on solid ground.

Sam was the eldest of four children, but as a teenager, he'd never shown much interest in the business. After his compulsory military service, Sam travelled around the world for several years. He returned home in order to start school, focusing on computer sciences. His first job experience was less than ideal—he'd gotten a job at an internet company but hated it and was fired less than a year later. It was at this point that he asked his parents if he could join the family business. They were torn; they wanted a successor but had doubts about Sam's ability to assume that role.

Michelle, in particular, was skeptical about the possibility that he would commit himself to working hard and learning the business inside out. Marvin wasn't sure that Sam would be able to learn the business, but he was willing to give it a try. Dorot's Next Generation expert, Tal Yahav, started to meet biweekly with Sam. Together they explored his career alternatives—might there be *something* else he wanted to do?—and finally came to the conclusion that joining the family business was what he genuinely wanted. They investigated his strengths, and working from that information, they prepared an educational program.

The program included course work in the subject matter, spread out over two years; the sequence of jobs he should perform in the business; and one-on-one meetings with a consultant in order to improve his leadership skills. Since then Sam and his parents have given lectures several times to family business audiences, detailing the process Sam has worked through and highlighting how well it has worked out for them.

Sam is now working in the business as a marketing manager, and he works well with both his parents and the other managers. Michelle's doubts about him have vanished, and his sister, who recently joined the business, considers him the "first among equals."

Understanding that the integration into the family business can be planned and enhanced is one of a parent's duties. While Sam certainly did his share in the success of the training program, it was his parents' encouragement, involvement, and willingness to finance it that made it possible.

Objective Feedback

It is almost impossible to give one's child authentic feedback on the quality of their work. They may not admit it when their child is working close to them, but in retrospect, all the seniors in our study said that they couldn't do it; their perspective was too skewed. Sadly, objective feedback is the one thing that successors in family businesses are most in need of. Their managers, peers, and employees don't dare give them candid feedback, and their parents are unable to do so. Their situation is a lot like driving a car without mirrors. They need an objective mentor, like an external board member or a consultant (or sometimes a manager within the business, though this is rare), to help them acquire an accurate perspective.

PLAN THE GIVING

Unlike many other countries, Israel does not have an inheritance tax, which means that people don't feel obligated to make any sort of coherent (tax-based) estate plan. Heads of families often find it easier or more convenient to simply say, "After my death, the survivors will deal with it the best they can. It's not my problem." While this is technically true, leaving such emotionally loaded decisions to a group of grieving siblings is unkind. I think parents owe it to their children to decide exactly how, when, and what they want to give to their children.

This will involve answering the following questions:

- Do they want to give equally or according to need?
- Do they want to give to all siblings jointly, or each one separately?
- Do they want to equip their children to support themselves, or do they want to actually support them (i.e., to give them a fish or a fishing rod)?
- What kind of strings do they intend to attach to their giving, and what strings are actually being attached?
- Which gifts do they want to give during their lifetime, and which after their death?
- Do the same rules apply to all kinds of giving?

The following story can clarify this last question.

I worked with one family that distinguished among three categories: self-development, starting one's own business, and gifts from parents. Each category was governed by different principles. Self-development was supported according to need. Financial support for starting a business was given after reviewing a business plan, and only as bank guarantees. Gifts from parents (such as houses, money, etc.), were given strictly equally to all children.

When the giving is not only planned, but also communicated to the successors, it allows the parents to hear their children out. It helps them to know what works and what causes anguish or jealousy, and to consider changes or other solutions. Contrary to some attorneys I meet, I believe that the giving plan is better communicated in advance, in order to save dispute after the parents' death.

CARE FOR CHILDREN WITH SPECIAL NEEDS

If your child cannot properly take care of themselves, parents are obliged to ensure that they have set up a trust or some other way of supporting their needs. Parents of people with special needs often give them shares, assuming that their siblings will make good decisions and that this will produce profits for all. In my opinion, however, it is wrong to make the financial support of a person with special needs dependent on the business decisions of their siblings. At Dorot, we work with a professional social worker who helps families assess how much money will actually be needed over the course of their child's life, enabling the family to set up an adequate trust.

Some parents feel that one or more of their children should be spared the responsibility of managing wealth, but they dislike the idea that they might treat one of their offspring differently from their siblings. This is understandable, as labeling someone as "unable to take care of their own wealth" has long-lasting repercussions. Even so, it is the parents' duty to see that the gift they make does not fall like a "meteor" (in Jay Hughes' terminology) into their child's life, and that the receiver has the skills necessary to manage their wealth, or has a professional support system in place to ensure that those finances are secured. Giving wealth to a person who cannot handle it would be like giving me an airplane as a gift. I don't know how to care for an airplane. I don't know what staff is needed, which professionals I should hire, what kind of hangar should be prepared, or anything else about airplanes except that flying in one is a sometimes convenient way to get somewhere. In short, I am unfit to have an airplane and would not appreciate being given one.

DEALING WITH COMPLEX FAMILIES

We frequently work with complex (sometimes called "blended") families and will doubtless continue to do so, as the divorce rate has gone up considerably throughout the Western world. We consider complex families to be families with second marriages and children from different parents. That gives rise to complexities with regard to continuity of the family enterprise and a new set of duties for the parents.

As a family becomes more complex—either through second marriages or step-children—the model of the Family Business System, as discussed in chapter 5, also grows in complexity. As shown in figure 5 below, the family circle inevitably splits in two. In the case of a second marriage, this split is seen in the divide between the first spouse and their children (i.e., the first family), and the second.

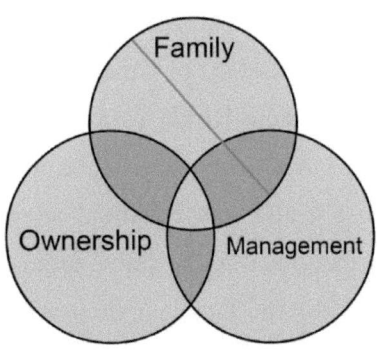

Figure 5. The Family Business System—blended families

Family separations and divisions are rife with potential areas of conflict, oftentimes tinged with bad feeling—and for good reason. Any significant age gap between sets of children may result in the elder children getting first crack at the family business, meaning they can therefore fill all the important roles long before the second set of kids has even considered their career options. It's easy for the younger set to feel that they've been unjustly denied their birthright, while the older set may discriminate against their younger half-siblings, citing their youth and inexperience in matters of business.

Another source of conflict has to do with differences in values and lifestyles between the two parts of the family. For instance, if one set of successors grew up while the founder was still struggling, and the second set was born into the founder's wealth, the first set will resent the second for having had everything handed to them, while the second set will resent the first for having more experience with the founder's business and being the natural successors.

This lack of empathy is plainest when the children view one another as potential rivals for the parent's wealth. True, it is a fact of life that when the parent starts a new family, it affects the assets that will one day pass to their successors. But in my experience, what turns this into a source of bitterness is the fact that the parent and their new spouse don't clearly explain the legal and financial realities of their arrangement to either set of children.

Parents who had a new family told me with frustration, "It's none of my children's business what I give to my spouse. It's my money and I can use it any way I want. I am entitled to my own happiness." This is true, but at the same time, parents should also assume responsibility for the fact that their actions have an impact on other members of their family. Not knowing where they stand puts the children in a highly uncertain position, which gives rise to animosity and conflict among siblings. A parent must take steps to mitigate any unintended consequences, or otherwise live with the resulting unhappy family.

I once worked with a family in which the father (who was in the second generation) had two distinct families and had never introduced them to each other. As they grew older, the children maintained that separation, as the older children were afraid that any contact they had with their father's new family would hurt their mother's feelings. I eventually was able to convince everyone (including the mothers) that it was in the interests of all the children to meet one another at least once, as they were all their father's heirs. The beginning of the meeting was quite tense, as the two sets of children eyed each other suspiciously, and the tension finally erupted when the son of the first wife pointed an accusing finger at his two half-siblings and said, "This is all your fault."

I was quite proud of one of the younger siblings, who answered in measured tones, "We are all victims of our father's choices. The way he handled this situation has hurt every one of us. Can't we all recognize we're in the same boat?"

I can't say that the two sets of siblings left the meeting as friends, but the ice had been broken. They all agreed that even if they would never be close, they could at least acknowledge one another's existence.

CONCLUSION

"What will happen to my family and my business when I am no longer here?" I've heard this fear from countless seniors. It keeps them up at night because unlike the business challenges they encountered throughout their careers, the future of the family enterprise is outside of their control. Loss of control is a hard thing for most people to accept, let alone personalities as tenacious as those of many founders. The fear can be crippling. Some of them opt out of dealing with it entirely, "This is none of my business. After my death, my successors will have to handle it." Others try to solve it through detailed legal documents, leaving them "in control from the grave," for many years to come. I would not recommend either of these extreme solutions.

Rather, based on parent and successor insights, this chapter is intended to suggest a format aimed at the responsible parent, an approach that lands somewhere between the two extremes described above.

Based on other families' experiences, the main duties of the seniors are:

1. Realize that ownership is a vocation that cannot be learned overnight.

2. Choose the next leader from among the siblings.

3. Avoid confusion between business leadership and parenthood.

4. Support the preparation process, with encouragement, involvement, and financial support.

5. Find someone who can provide the necessary objective feedback.

6. Plan your giving, and communicate the plan.

7. Make appropriate arrangements for children with special needs.

8. Assume responsibility for the repercussions of your personal family life for the sake of your children.

While this list is certainly demanding, it attempts to turn parental obligations into manageable responsibilities. The above duties can be fulfilled, whether you are affectionate or not, and whether you have free time or not. Remember, from here on out, it is up to your offspring to make the best of what you have given them.

CHAPTER 8

Work with Your Natural Partners

Acquire for yourself a friend; and judge every person in their favor.
Ethics of the Fathers (Pirkei Avot), 1;6

Although I was an only child and therefore very close to my parents, life in the kibbutz taught me to rely on my Gen Peer group for most of my daily life. The hours of my day—first at school, then at work, and finally my leisure time—were mostly spent with my friends. I learned that although my parents would try to be familiar with my world and concerns, it was really my peers who shared my challenges and joys. I learned to trust them. So, it was no surprise that when I finally decided to leave the kibbutz at the age of twenty, it was a colleague from my Gen Peer group who found me my first job outside. He helped me to start my new life out of the "commune," and I remained forever thankful to him.

With this background, it was little wonder that I felt very lonely in my first years in the US. I was a young career woman and a young mother. I was far away from my support system and felt alone. When my son was quite young—young enough to need more or less constant supervision—my husband and I found ourselves in a bit of a pickle. The life of a young family is one of constant and careful scheduling, and because we were both working, we'd grown accustomed to relying on each other to step in whenever our professional schedules conflicted with our childcare needs. But professional lives are rarely flexible enough to make space for a child.

So, one day, when my husband was away at a conference, I found myself forced to choose between an important meeting with a client and making sure that my infant son was safe. I'd imagined that someday this circumstance would arise, but I hadn't expected it would come quite so soon, and I had no plan.

I'd resigned myself to calling the client to reschedule—potentially losing their business—when I glanced out my office window and saw the straw hat of my neighbor, Sarah, bobbing along the top of the fence that divided our gardens, as she watered her tomato plants. Sarah was a stay-at-home mother with two children, the youngest being only a year older than my son. We knew each other enough to exchange smiles in the market, but I hadn't had much time for friends recently.

I began to think that maybe that should change.

It was the work of a moment. A simple exchange—she'd look after my child for the afternoon, and I'd watch her kids the next time she and her husband went out together—and somehow we formed a bond that has outlasted our babysitting needs. As the years passed, we've spent a great deal of time in each other's homes, leaning on each other when trouble struck, and celebrating with each other when everything went right. In seeking an ally against the whims of circumstance, I found a friend.

Allies—partners in work and in life—are an important part of every enterprise. The founding generation is usually just one person (or one couple)—one vision for the future, one driving force of talent and enthusiasm—but in the second and third generations, all that creativity and expertise ends up being distributed over multiple owners. The bond between vision and execution is stretched as those people pursue their own paths, but business prosperity and family harmony are inextricably linked to that bond. To keep their business healthy, owners must be an effective team of partners: they must trust one another, communicate clearly and kindly, understand the reality of the challenges that face them, deal with disagreements with tact and wisdom, and be able to affect the decisions made by the group without falling to squabbling and personal ambition. It's not an easy task. It takes conscious effort, training, and dedication.

Even when the relationships are complex, successfully managing this partnership is possible. The Haniel Group in Germany was founded in 1756 and is still in the hands of the Haniel family. Today, there are more than 650 shareholders, all of whom are family members. They adhere to an elaborate system that includes business meetings and family vacations, as well as an exhaustive course in management and leadership training known as the Haniel Academy, which every future shareholder is expected to go through.

But most of the families I work with aren't hundreds of years old. Most families are working through the difficulties of transitioning from the first generation to the second, or from the second to the third. And most families hope to transfer ownership to every member of the next generation, viewing the option of a single-heir path as something that would disrupt the family dynamic—something that fails in their most basic ambitions. But many of these families may not realize the amount of effort that must go into a multiple partnership, that these relationships call for extensive preparation and constant investment. From time to time I run into a case where the alternative option of handing down ownership to only one of the siblings would work better, but that is my outsider observation of the situation, and eventually I try to help the family fulfill its own plan.

If you want a healthy, growing business, complexity is inevitable. And important. As one leader of such a family once said: "We create successful global partnerships in our companies because we are used to handling complexities. We do that within the family all the time."

So, who are these partners that a family member must work with? In whom, among all of one's relatives, would you want to invest your time? I feel that the clearest answer will always be the members of one's own generation—the people called one's "Gen Peers." For a variety of reasons, these are your "natural partners."

Every generation grows up in a set of circumstances common to them but not to the previous generation. Millennials grew up with the internet, for example, while baby boomers grew up tied to a landline. These circumstances color the way a generation thinks, the way it communicates. And no matter how enlightened you are, or how excellent you believe your communication skills to be, it will always be easier to find common ground with your own generation. Moreover, the transition from founders to the second generation usually creates a mental gap. Grubman and Jaffe[8] describe it as the gap between immigrants and natives in the land of wealth. Bridging this mental gap is almost impossible. A like-minded mentality exists between successors that founders have no part in, meaning that lateral partnerships within a generation group can be much more fruitful than vertical partnerships between members of different generations.

That said, working with one's natural partners should not be done in place of building a dialogue with the senior generation.

---

[8] James Grubman and Dennis T. Jaffe, "Immigrants and Natives to Wealth: Understanding Clients Based on Their Wealth Origins," *Journal of Financial Planning* (July 2007): 46–54.

Intergenerational cooperation is essential for the overall success of the enterprise. But relying on one's peers allows the younger generation to carry out that dialogue from a position of security, enabling it to be as constructive as possible.

Combining family relations with business decisions is never easy It is certainly easier to maintain good relationships when adult family members see each other around the festive dinner table, when everyone looks happy and rested and is on their best behavior. It is a different thing entirely to see parents or siblings in moments of stress or fatigue, when the mistakes are flying thick and fast, and people are doing things they'll later regret.

Even worse, the old tensions and rivalries do not have an expiration date. In the Solomon family, the third generation was already running the business: Marc was CFO, Lidia was VP of Marketing, and Jonathan was COO, in charge of operations. Each represented a different branch of the family. As competition from China grew, the business struggled, and the cost of labor rose. But at board meetings, their parents (the second generation) would spend their time arguing about why the founding father (who had been deceased for twenty-five years) had invited Aron, the son in-law, into the business: Was it out of appreciation for Aron's potential contribution or because the founder's daughter might not be financially secure otherwise? And moreover, people were jealous of the brother who served as CEO. And people didn't like how "snobby" one of the family members was. And there was a years-old loan dispute that had never been properly resolved. The problems between the various siblings kept mounting, and as often happens, their animosity was fed by many factors.

When a situation explodes and a fight breaks out, it is often difficult to understand why people are really fighting. Things like ownership, money, failure, jealousy, or even what one grandchild said to the other at a recent family event can all get mixed up in a vortex of shouting and finger-pointing. In the third generation, Marc, Lidia, and Jonathan did their best to leave the family fights aside and collaborate on business matters. But in their personal conversations, I often saw the animosity of their parents poisoning their attitudes toward one another.

There's an old Jewish family joke:

"What do you call a cousin?"

"The son of that woman we do not speak to."

Rivalries are one of the easiest things to pass down through generations. This joke makes a good point, but Jewish families are not alone in this tendency.

Over the course of my career, I've learned that the family tree can be seen in two ways: vertically and horizontally. Figure 6 below shows a vertical treatment. Branches grow apart and may eventually be cut from the tree.

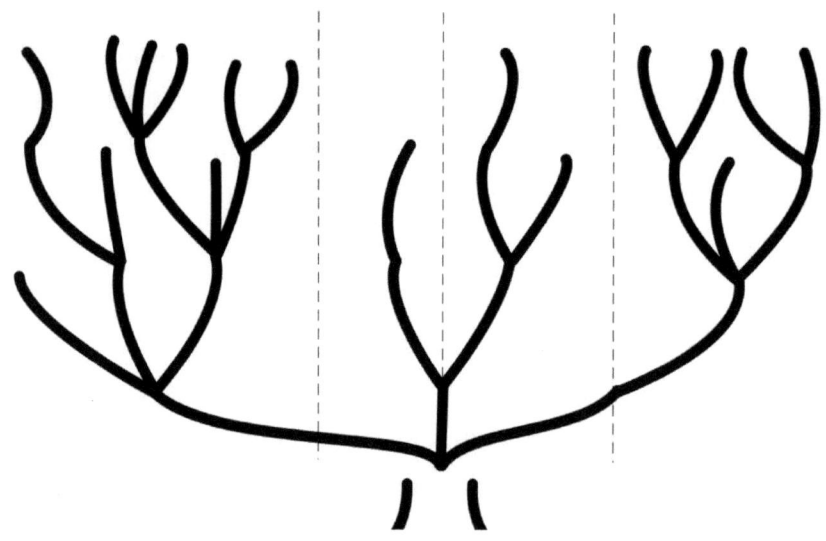

Figure 6. Vertical family tree

Figure 7. Horizontal family tree

But in figure 7, the tree is considered horizontally. It focuses on the many layers of the generations. In time, each generation becomes a "circle" in the tree trunk, indicating the age of the tree.

The vertical method of trimming the tree has some obvious advantages. It keeps ownership in the hands of fewer people, preserving the ability to make fast decisions and stay flexible.

Most of the families I work with prefer to remain together. They see "trimming" the tree as a sign of failure. But whether it is right or wrong to trim the family tree, one thing is certain. Trimming the tree as the end result of a bitter fight is detrimental to the family and the business. The Solomon family ended up in a bitter split. The younger generation couldn't keep the senior generation's drive for family feuds at bay, and they eventually became embroiled in a lawsuit, so no one had the energy to devote to urgent business matters. Sadly, the motto of another family's matriarch ("We fight only with competitors. Within the family we are always united.") was not part of their family's legacy.

Considering the family tree via the horizontal perspective encourages the formation of a working partnership *within* the next generation. When that generation, as a team of future owners, initiates the dialogue with their seniors, they get the seniors to consider their issues from a constructive and responsible point of view, rather than from the perspective of old rivalries and irrelevant bickering.

However, creating a partnership with your Gen Peers is easier said than done. In the Kelman family, there are four family branches with nine third-generation cousins. The business had been founded by Grandpa Stuart in Europe and had since spread into different European countries, along with Israel and the US. As a result, the nine cousins do not share a mother tongue. They all speak English, but it is no one's first language, and no one is completely comfortable in it. This means that the communication between these Gen Peers lacks intuitiveness and fluency that many other Gen Peer groups enjoy.

Nevertheless, the cousins soldiered on and recently decided to invest in family meetings and to educate themselves on the process of what it takes to be future owners. The most important part of their decision as a group was the realization that an important aspect of this preparation would be related to their partnership. They recognized that they would have to work hard to identify common values, define a shared vision for the future, practice communication, and create trust and respect within the group.

I started talking about "natural partners" because high-tech start-up companies were using the term, and I wanted to acknowledge that the culture of entrepreneurship had undergone a generational shift. In an article[9] published in 2010, my colleagues and I evaluated some of the differences between high-tech and traditional entrepreneurs. We found that there were significant differences in the family histories of these two groups, as well as differences in their education level and in their relationship with the enterprise they created. Most importantly, we noted a difference in the way these two generational groups relied on community. The "old economy" entrepreneur was usually a loner, starting their business alone, or with their spouse. These entrepreneurs were poor partners and generally less skilled at teaching their children how partnerships work. High-tech entrepreneurs, on the other hand, seem to create their ventures in conjunction with their "crew." The crew is usually a group of old friends, with relationships that go back to their early days in the military service or college. They move together from one venture to the next, and their partnership stays stable. They would not consider moving to a new venture without their "natural partners."

I think of Gen Peers as being more like the high-tech crew than their founding parents' lone entrepreneurship. If we think of Gen Peers as a potential "crew" of successors, we can come to several conclusions:

1. Gen Peers have to create their own partnership. Parents can teach them many things, but not partnership.

2. Gen Peers have to detach themselves from their parents' issues and rivalries. As Lea, a fourth-gen member, told her cousin Edith: "The fact that your father and my father are

---

9 Orenia Yaffe-Yanai, Tamar Milo, and Gilat Kaplan, "High-Tech Entrepreneurs versus Entrepreneurs in Traditional Industries: Similarities and Differences in Family Portraits and Passion Quests," in *Handbook of Research on High-Technology Entrepreneurs,* eds. Ayala Malach-Pines and Mustafa F. Özbilgin (Cheltenham, UK: Edward Elgar Publishing, 2010), 42–56.

not on speaking terms is none of my business. If I can work well with you, and we have a shared interest, I'll do so. I'll let my father deal with his own issues."

3. The flow of communication within the family must undergo a gradual shift from a **solar system model**—in which information flows from a child to the parent, and from the parent to all other children, with little direct communication among the children (see chapter 1)—to a **free floating model** as the successors become young adults.

On the other hand, when siblings or cousins create a working partnership with their Gen Peers, the flow of communication is much more direct, as shown in figure 8 below.

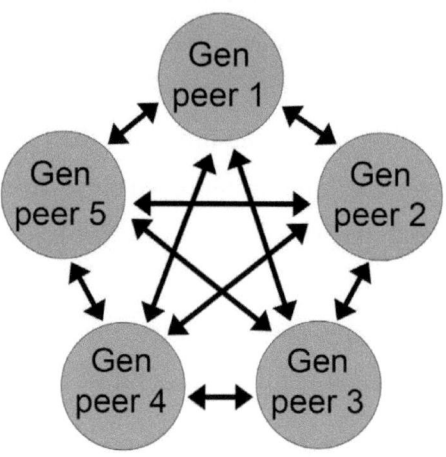

Figure 8. Free floating model

4. By leaving the solar system model, Gen Peers gradually shift into a universe in which there is no authority that dictates the value of any particular action. They may have come

from a situation in which the patriarch was responsible for these judgments, but now the Gen Peers themselves must make their own decisions—usually through discussion and joint decision-making.

Whenever I facilitate this process, I find that I am expected to be a judge, or arbitrator, but that is not my role, and I have little interest in who is "right." (I believe that when it comes to families, being "right" does not help. What would one do after they had been proclaimed to be right? If rivalry and animosity persist, being right does no one any good.) The shift to a free floating model takes Gen Peers into a realm that values acceptance and inclusion, rather than judgment.

5. Even after a sibling partnership has been formed, the shift from the solar system model to the free floating model requires practice. Old habits are hard to shake. When the free floating model applies to cousins, it is even more difficult to get it going. Our work with groups of cousins typically happens over a long period of time, as we are helping them to practice open communication and teamwork.

SIBLING RIVALRIES

It would be naïve or unrealistic to not recognize the role of sibling rivalry as a barrier to Gen Peer partnerships. Miri and Bill were the two older siblings in a family of four children. They had been working in their parents' business for more than ten years. Miri had taken over as CEO and Bill worked as the VP of marketing and sales. They had carried most (if not all) of the responsibility for the business but felt that the family treated them like employees who had no influence on decision-making. To address this grievance, the family decided to create a Family Agreement to spell out the structure of their authority and attend to the gradual transfer of shares and their salaries. But despite the fact that this process was designed to solve their problem, we consistently found ourselves stuck in the weeds.

Every time we got close to an agreement, Miri and Bill erupted in an argument that made moving forward impossible. I finally realized that the rivalry between the two, baked into their relationship since childhood, made it impossible for them to trust each other. As long as they thought of themselves as rivals, they could not be partners, and the Family Agreement could go nowhere. I suggested that they work on their relationship with the help of our Next Generation Consultant Tal Yahav, and their meetings shed light on the differences between them but focused mainly on their common values and shared vision for the future. This emotional realignment created the foundation for an inspirational partnership. They were finally able to define a shared code of conduct and to specify ways in which they could creatively solve any unforeseen problems. After several months, Miri and Bill felt that they had transformed the way they viewed each other, moving from "he does everything in his power to take my place and upset me" to "she's a team member who has unique strengths, and who can complement my abilities." They could now trust each other, and they felt that together they could face the demands of the business and the family. As Miri put it, "Not only can I now see Bill as my partner, I even want him to come to my house with his family, to spend the weekend."

GEN-PEER FORUM

Being in a family business often means feeling lonely. Over the years, I've met so many family members who thought that they were the only ones in the world experiencing the dilemma of wealth, ownership, and generation gap. They felt they were caught up in a situation that no one could understand or solve. This feeling may be magnified for the next-gen members working in their family business. Contrary to the way they are often portrayed in films and the media, most of them are not spoiled, unqualified young people. Rather, they are highly educated young adults who have been promoted to senior positions on a fast track. They quickly assume a great deal of responsibility, with relatively limited experience. To make the process even more challenging, most family-owned enterprises simply don't have well-established structures to serve as support systems to these well-meaning young people. They are typically left to weather the storm of expectations and responsibilities entirely on their own.

It is for them that we formed the Gen-Peer Forum, a group of next-gen members from different enterprises who come together to learn about the responsibilities and challenges of finding their place within a family business and serving as champions within their families.

Gen-Peer Forums may include successors who live far away from each other, so we often plan for two retreats in which members can meet in person, while the rest of the meetings take place over the internet or via video conference.

Eileen was thirty-six years old when she joined the Gen-Peer Forum. She was the oldest daughter of an entrepreneur who began with a small-scale construction company. The construction company expanded until it was a leading company in its field. Eileen graduated with a law degree and completed her practice in a large law firm. She then joined her father's company, in which she took charge of the legal department and customer service.

Eileen was industrious, hardworking, and ambitious. She was eager to learn how to communicate well with her dad, to find ways to introduce changes in the business practices, and to have a safe place to air some of her frustrations with her siblings.

In the Gen-Peer Forum, Eileen met, for the first time, with young adults in situations similar to hers. The group facilitator introduced rules of conduct, which made the forum a safe place to discuss discreet dilemmas, but Eileen was a competitive person. It took her a few monthly meetings to realize that this group was not about competition but about sharing and collaborating. She gradually learned to trust her peers with her most pressing problems at work and to incorporate their suggestions into her practice.

Eileen's group chose to continue to meet for a second and third year. Their mutual support now happens between the meetings as well as during them. More significant is the fact that since Eileen began using this outlet for support and idea-sharing, her father promoted her to a VP position and considers her work to be excellent. She even successfully negotiated a raise with her father, a challenge that she had initially considered to be insurmountable.

For Eileen and her peers, the Gen-Peer Forum is unlike any other group they belong to. "It is a place where I can explore my role in the family and in the business," said one member. Another one said, "Listening to my colleagues' personal situations gives me perspective and patience. It makes me less judgmental and a more forgiving person." A third commented that "being a part of a group helps me understand what I contribute to the family group." And a fourth noted that "between the meetings, I find myself waiting for the next meeting, so I can share with my peers the recent drama in my family business." The perpetual sense of loneliness these young people felt has been replaced by a sense of empathetic comradery.

CONCLUSION

Working with one's Gen Peers does not mean being "against" the senior generation. Rather, it is about creating a dialogue between generations from a position of commitment and self-awareness. In earlier chapters, we've discussed the duties of the next generation: recommit and reinvent. Because modern society is complex, global, and rapid, it requires collaboration and teamwork. Modern breakthroughs are almost never the province of the sole entrepreneur—teamwork is the way forward, the path to progress. If we are to encourage development and discovery, we must support the development of team-building and partnership skills. Gen Peer partnership should be part of this development process.

A word about the implications of this process on parents: Seniors seem to respond well to the formation of effective Gen Peer partnerships. They intuitively feel the sense of growing mastery and responsibility that come with the development of a team. Once they know that the business they built will be in safe hands, it becomes easier for them to let go of its power and authority. Moreover, building these teams usually falls in line with parents' overall goals of familial harmony. They always wanted their children to work well together. They may not have known how to make it happen, but they are nevertheless overjoyed to see that dream come true.

CHAPTER 9

Create Tangible Results

One whose wisdom is greater than his deeds, what is he comparable to? To a tree with many branches and few roots; comes a storm and uproots it, and turns it on its face ... But one whose deeds are greater than his wisdom, to what is he compared? To a tree with many roots and few branches, whom all the storms in the world cannot budge from its place.

Ethics of the Fathers (Pirkei Avot), 3:17

My country is not blessed with much rain, but when the rains come, they pour hard, over a short period of time, and create local floods. Water gets into houses, blocks traffic, and causes all kinds of damage. After each such storm there is an outcry for improving the infrastructure, in order to prevent the same thing to happen next time. But the next day, the sun shines, everything dries up, and the need for better infrastructure is forgotten. By the time the next storm arrives, it is too late to prevent the damage.

Michelle called me one day, after years of animosity and rivalry between her and her sister. They were both the successors of their father, who founded a flourishing real estate company. Michelle worked with her father, but despite that close relationship, she felt that he still favored her sister. Over the years, she accumulated evidence that proved, according to her, her father's bias and her sister's unfair behavior toward her. She became obsessed, and her immediate family suffered for it.

The situation came to an open crisis when her father told the sisters that he had prepared a will, without telling them its content. Michelle contacted me, asking that I help them dialogue and reach an agreement. However, she demanded that a lie detector test be included in my diagnosis. Obviously, I refused, explaining to her that this was not a tool I used in my practice. I went on to say that if they did not solve the issue amicably, it would end up in court. "At least in court, I shall have an opportunity to meet my sister," was Michelle's reply. I let it go. Several months later, the father passed away. All hell broke loose, and as predicted, the case wound up in legal traction.

Unlike the situation with Michelle and her sister, for the D'Arrone family, the situation could be saved. The mother wanted to start a process of writing a Family Agreement. I met with the entire family to present the process, but they decided to put it off, arguing that they were too busy with urgent business challenges. A year later, the mother called me again, saying there was a crisis with the oldest son. Now, they were all willing to take the time and invest what it took to put together the Family Agreement. It turned out that the crisis was directly related to policies and decision-making processes. Discussions during the creation of a Family Agreement resolved the issue and restored communication between the generations.

Too often, families tend to put off planning and rule writing until something triggers a sudden need for it. That trigger can be dramatic—the resignation or dismissal of a family member, or an acrimonious argument between two siblings—and it's usually not something that can be easily resolved. Sometimes, as in the case of Michelle and her sister, it is simply too late. At other times, crisis intervention may be helpful. But once a consultant steps in and resolves the immediate problem by creating a space for the family to discuss the triggering issue, the need for the consultant's services feels less pressing. Soon the family members become too busy to schedule their next appointment, and after a while, family participation in the planning process simply falls away.

I try to warn families in advance that this eventual disinterest is a danger. Dealing only with an acute problem and ignoring its underlying structural causes is just like taking antibiotics up until the point where your throat feels sort of OK, and then throwing away the rest of the treatment.

As soon as I see family members begin to lose interest in the process, I know that it's my job as a consultant to push the project forward. I know that if the process is not completed, the next time an issue comes up—and that time *will* come—the family will not be properly equipped to handle it. Even if they have a clearer picture of their family dynamic, even if they have become more aware of what it takes to run the system smoothly, they still haven't anchored these achievements in written documents and long-lasting procedures.

They have nothing to cement the agreements they've reached within the family or with the shareholders. Their recollections may be helpful in the short run, and may allow the family to handle current issues, but over time those verbal agreements will lose their potency. Memories will get fuzzy. Eventually, everyone remembers an agreement differently, and without those documents—that tangible record of what has been agreed upon—the same problems that caused the crisis in the first place will inevitably resurface.

Therefore, all the planning and difficult conversations within the family won't be a good enough protection, if the results aren't written down. Written documents are essential for the healthy progress of a family enterprise, and their primary purpose is to ensure clarity, order, and transparency.

Real change requires tangible results. These results come in three categories of deliverables that a consultant can guide a family to create: Governance structures, policies, and processes. These products should be open and transparent, visible enough to family members to be a statement of the way in which the family manages its affairs. Their visibility gives them a longevity that usually serves to stabilize the family–enterprise interfaces for as long as that business exists. They become part of the family legacy.

GOVERNANCE STRUCTURES

Each of the three circles in the Family Business System diagram (see figure 2 in chapter 5) has a body that manages it: the *Business* is governed by the management team, the *Ownership* is run by the board of directors (BOD), and the *Family* is governed by the Family Council (FC).

Not all family businesses have all of these structures in place. When a business is young, decisions are mostly made at the dinner table by the founder, or by the parents. But as the business grows and non-family managers join the team, management meetings become essential to cooperation among departments, to gathering and distributing information, and to making decisions. A fascinating recent study by Jaffe[10] suggests that when it comes to the order in which governance structures are established, the management of the business always comes first. The distinction between deliberations

---

10 Dennis T. Jaffe, *Good Fortune: Building a Hundred Year Family Enterprise* (Milton, MA: Wise Counsel Research, August 2013).

within the management team and decisions made by owners comes much later.

The Board of Directors (BOD)

The BOD represents the owners. Although privately held companies are not legally required to have one, a growing number of family-held companies elect to have formal boards, with or without independent (external) board members. The owners of many privately held companies feel that having external members on the board better allows it to fulfill its main governance role—avoiding conflicts between the family members' family and the business roles—while preserving unity among the family members.[11] Another study conducted on the boards of family-held enterprises indicated that the balance between their advising and controlling roles changes depending on which generation of the family runs the enterprise. The study showed that the need for advice decreases from the first to the second generation and rises again in third and subsequent generations. On the other hand, the need for firm control on the part of the board increases over the generations, in parallel to the number of family directors.[12]

Michael Strauss was one of the first family business owners in Israel to establish a BOD with non-family directors. He started it in the 1980s, when the enterprise was relatively small, and the cost of these board members was a noticeable financial burden. Even so, he insisted on appointing to the board capable, experienced people

---

11 Suzanne Lane, Joseph Astrachan, Andrew Keyt, and Kristi McMillan, "Guidelines for Family Business Boards of Directors," *Family Business Review* 19, no. 2 (2006): 147–167.

12 Yannick Bammens, Wim Voordeckers, and Anita Van Gils, "Board of Directors in Family Firms: A Generational Perspective," *Small Business Economics* 31, no. 2 (2008): 163–180.

from his own industry—new voices with external perspectives who could add value to BOD deliberations. He told them explicitly that he expected them to argue with him whenever they thought he was wrong. As he explained it in a lecture, their presence also meant that the board meetings were required to have a set agenda, with materials prepared in advance and sent out to all board members. The addition of these non-family directors forced the BOD to become more formal and better organized. Thirty years later, his family business is a global conglomerate, an achievement that Strauss attributes in part to the board of directors.

Besides the economic contribution, the organization inherent in the development of a BOD can have unanticipated benefits. For instance, my clients Evelyne and Don were siblings who had inherited a small tool manufacturing company from their father. Don was in charge of manufacturing and development, while Evelyne took care of sales and finance. They usually made decisions jointly, in an informal way. When one of them opposed an idea, the idea was simply put aside. I've known many families who make decisions according to the same principle, and owners tend to gravitate toward this style of decision-making because it maintains family harmony (usually at the expense of innovation, but that's a conversation for another time).

As Evelyne approached her sixty-third birthday, she grew tired of working so hard, and she tried to convince Don to sell the business. However, before they could find a buyer, Evelyne's youngest son Shawn voiced a surprising interest in taking on the business and becoming the successor. This development overjoyed Evelyne and Don, but it brought to the fore a few issues they hadn't really thought about, including Shawn's readiness for the position (which was minimal), the position of his cousin Ed (who worked in the business but didn't know whether he could be a partner with Shawn and his siblings), and most important, Evelyne and Don's future contribution to the company.

It had become obvious to everyone that if Shawn took over the business, Evelyne and Don would not want to step away entirely. They had spent their entire lives within the walls of the production hall and were not sure whether they could find meaningful activities outside of it. Moreover, the last thing their successors wanted was to lose the experience and expertise the two siblings had accumulated. After all, their time running the business made their knowledge and perspective priceless. But on the other hand, they also knew that Shawn wouldn't be able to establish his own authority within the company if his mother and uncle stayed on.

The solution was a board of directors. For the first time in the company's forty-five years of operation, an official board of directors was established. Its role was to be mainly one of advice but also of control. The Family Agreement (which we'll discuss later) specified that Evelyne, Ed, Shawn, and Don would become board members. It also specified which decisions should be made only by the BOD, and that the board should convene at least four times a year.

The process hasn't been seamless. One day, well into the reorganization process, I received a concerned phone call from Shawn. He told me that since Evelyne and Don were no longer active managers, he had expected to move them out of the office they'd shared for forty years, but he couldn't seem to bring himself to ask them to do so. He felt that it was important for them to continue having an office to come to whenever they visited the plant. I suggested that he leave them their old office but change the sign on the door to "Office of the Board." Shawn could take an empty room down the hall and transform it into the office of the CEO. Shawn loved the solution: It was respectful to the senior generation, while still being true to the new direction of the company.

After three years of work and steadfast devotion to the process, the system is working beautifully. Shawn is the CEO, and he has hired an external production manager. His cousin Ed is in charge of QA. Evelyne and Don show up occasionally, but mainly for board meetings—they're both too busy with their volunteer work and travels to be involved in the day-to-day workings of the company. Don had feared that he would miss coming into the office every day, but after taking the time to adjust, he's happy with the way he's spending his time. He doesn't feel at all irrelevant. When Evelyne and Don retire from the board, Shawn and his siblings (who have also become shareholders) hope to be able to bring on some external board members, who could bring in knowledge about finances, marketing, and strategic thinking. The future of their company seems to grow brighter by the day.

The Family Council (FC)

The prosperity of a family business isn't just dependent on the management of the business itself. Family harmony is crucial to maintaining a supportive environment in which managers can perform and all members of the family can thrive, whether they work in the business or not. In many founding families, the work of managing the family life often falls to the mother. She arranges the family dinners, organizes family vacations, and oftentimes is the one who represents the family at philanthropic events. She works in an informal way, and as long as the children are young, her task is relatively simple. However, as her children grow and build their own nuclear families, her work becomes increasingly complex. Newcomers to the family hail from different backgrounds and have different values, habits, and needs. The children of these new families are diverse in age and have different needs. Something as simple as organizing a picnic may reveal unexpected challenges and become a source of dissatisfaction for some members of the family.

As the family continues to grow, the task becomes even harder. When a family has a third or fourth generation, the group has usually spread out over the globe and may see one another only infrequently. It is impossible for anyone to know all the family members intimately, and the old founders, who held everyone together, may no longer be alive—meaning their legacy is at risk of extinction. It's at this time of incredible complexity that families often decide they need a Family Council.

A Family Council is a governing body that represents the family circle of the Family Business System diagram. In some cases, it is the highest authority within the organization, the group that elects family shareholder representatives for the board of directors. In other cases, it operates in parallel to the BOD and deals with matters such as education for the next generation, family legacy, philanthropy, and family gatherings, among myriad other duties.

For instance, Diane was married to a third-generation successor in a family enterprise. I'd been working with her for some time, and she was a regular participant in a group of other family business mothers, led by myself and my colleague at Dorot. One day she arrived at the group meeting, obviously distraught. She told us that she and her husband had hoped to take the whole family abroad on vacation, but that an impossible burden had fallen on her shoulders. In organizing the trip for everyone—already a challenging endeavor—she was beset on all sides by the family's frustrating requests and endless complaints. "All we're doing is giving everyone a gift," she said. "Why is the whole thing turning out to be such a mess?" The members of the group, all of them mothers of families like hers, identified with her but were also able to ask probing questions ("How did you present the idea to the next generation?" "What were your and your husband's goals, to begin with?" "Why did you take all the organization upon yourself?" "Why is it important to you that all of you stay together during the entire vacation?") and give her feedback. She listened and processed.

When she left the meeting, she sent the following message to the family WhatsApp group:

> *My dear family, Dad and I would like to invite you all on a family vacation from August 1 to August 20 in Tuscany, Italy. You are all invited to join us for some of the time, or for the whole time, as you wish. I'll be happy to make the travel arrangements for whoever would like me to. Please let me know, or make your own way. I wish us all a great vacation, all of us together and each of us individually. We'll coordinate our expectations later.*
>
> *With love and respect,*
>
> *Mom and Dad*

The vacation was a success—and in the wake of that success, Diane realized that the family needed a body that could handle such tasks. Luckily, her children and their cousins were working at the same time on putting together a Family Agreement that also called for the establishment of a Family Council (FC). They decided that the FC would comprise two second-generation members, two third-generation members, and two spouses of either generation. The FC would be charged with organizing a yearly family weekend, a philanthropic project that would commemorate the founding grandparents, and a draft of a Family Statement that would explain what their extended family stood for. In addition, the FC would maintain transparency within the family, which meant creating a platform for announcing important developments in the family and the business, communicating FC decisions, and deciding what should be communicated and whatnot.

Family Councils are unique as the families they represent. Since it is a private creation and not subject to public regulation, an FC is designed to meet the specific needs of its extended family members. Because no family is identical to any other, every Family Council I've worked with has been different from the ones that came before it. That said, there are a few characteristics shared by every successful Family Council:

1. They provide a forum for the issues that don't fit in the management meeting or the BOD to be discussed and resolved. (Different types of issues have different platforms for discussions—in other words, the birthday party of the oldest grandson does not need to be discussed at the management meeting.)

2. Interested parties (such as groups of senior and junior generations, or spouses) are represented, allowing them to have an impact on subjects that relate to them, while not requiring them to voice an opinion on matters that concern the ownership or the management team of the enterprise. For instance, in one family I worked with, the daughter-in-law stormed into the founders' home one day, demanding that the son-in-law be fired from his management position. Possibly, if this family had already established its board of directors and its family council, the daughter-in-law would have known which areas she can

interfere with and which would be wholly inappropriate. She would also have had a forum in which she could raise her concerns without having to storm into the home of her in-laws.

3. They increase everybody's awareness of the importance of family unity and of the challenge of managing a multi-generational, multi-branch family. This awareness, invariably brings up issues like legacy and future shareholder education.

WRITTEN DOCUMENTS

Family Agreements

More than two decades ago, when I began working with families in business, most of my clients came to me in times of crisis: a son had entered the business but was doing a poor job; a daughter had threatened not to let her parents see their grandchildren; the business was performing poorly; and so on. But over time, a cultural awareness has developed of the challenges inherent in maintaining a family business, together with the benefits it brings. So today more families come to me saying, "All is well for now. The business is doing well, and our family is happy. But we know that if we do not set our policies now, something may go wrong in the future." These families come to create their Family Agreements.

Family Agreements come in many shapes and forms. Some are written as inspirational statements for future generations, while others are written as legal contracts. Each document is tailor-made for the family that created it. Sometimes they end up being called a Family Constitution, or a Family Charter, but regardless of what they are called, they all fulfill the same function: they are written policies that govern how members and governing bodies of the Family, Ownership, and Business interact with one another.

Heads of families fantasize, sometimes, that they will come up with these rules on their own and that everyone will abide by them. But in order to be long lasting, these documents must be a group effort, and the process of developing them must also be tailor-made for each family. I've had families all sit down together to discuss every section.

At the same time, there are situations in which the sheer size of the family makes it impossible to involve everyone. In those cases (usually large, multi-branch families), we try to encourage the use of a representative form of democracy—an elected steering committee, with representatives from every branch and generation—to prepare the draft. But I've also seen cases in which the younger generation took it upon itself to prepare a draft and then presented it to the senior generation. There is as much variation in the process as there is in the finished document, but in the end the final Family Agreement will always be the result of deep comprehension and agreement among the entire family. Even the in-laws, who in many cases are not invited to participate in the preparation of the agreement, are nevertheless invited to read the final draft and make comments. For a document to have the power to govern everyone, without any enforcement mechanism, everyone must know what it says and agree to abide by it.

People often ask me if an attorney is involved in the preparation of a Family Agreement, and the answer is positive, but not straightforward. Obviously, the agreement has to be in line with the legal system of the country in which it is executed, but even if there is only one legal system involved, one has to make sure that the agreement is in line with other legal documents, such as shareholders' wills, company documents, and prenuptial agreements. That's why I always work in collaboration with an attorney. I willingly stick with the family's trusted attorney; but in some cases, family members prefer to separate their corporate issues from family matters and prefer to work with a different lawyer.

In these cases, I ask the family to choose from a list of lawyers I've worked with before and know I can trust—mostly corporate lawyers who also understand family business issues and are familiar with the Family Agreement process. For most families, the lawyer enters the picture after the draft of the agreement is completed and makes sure that everything is legally feasible. I have had a few cases in which the family needed an expert legal opinion to decide how their processes should be shaped, and in those instances, we invited the attorney to be present during the discussions so they could give advice.

Because Family Agreements have become a cornerstone in the continuity process, they deserve a separate chapter. Chapter 10 details the topics that are addressed and provides examples of how various families chose to handle issues.

Wills

Once the Family Agreement is in place, to avoid contradictions, all other official documents must be synchronized to match it. I do most of my work in a country that does not have inheritance tax, and as a result, many people don't bother with estate planning. For them, the Family Agreement may be the first opportunity to think about wealth distribution and future planning, meaning that many of my clients embark on the mission of making a will only after the Family Agreement had been completed. Those who had already created a will then make sure that it is congruent with the Family Agreement.

Naturally, legal documents must be written according to the law of the country in which the family and the enterprise are based.

Prenuptial Agreements

Whenever a family member begins to discuss matters relating to the transfer of shares and assets to the next generation, the issue of prenuptial agreements invariably comes up. Regardless of whether parents want to impose prenup agreements on their children, most of them want to protect shares and assets from leaving the family's ownership. They know that without legal protection, like a prenup or a trust, the divorce or death of a family member could result in part of the assets ending up outside of the family.

There are pros and cons to prenups. James E. Hughes Jr., together with Massenzio and Whitaker,[13] discusses the complexity of this issue at length with some suggestions for how to discuss it within the family. The ease with which a family can discuss and decide upon this issue is very much related to the family's values and personal history. I've often found that the younger generation is more comfortable discussing the possible necessity of a prenup.

If the family decides that prenups are important, it is better if they are set as a rule that applies to everyone, rather than a special case. It is also recommended that it is presented to future spouses as a family or parent requirement rather than as the initiative of the son or daughter. Naturally, it is better to have the prenup agreed to and signed before the wedding, as everything becomes much more complex and sensitive after years of life together. If the question of such an agreement comes up after the couple has been married for some time, it is wiser—and certainly less fraught—to explore other

---

13 James E. Hughes Jr., Susan E. Messenzio, and Keith Whitaker, *Complete Family Wealth* (Hoboken, NJ: Wiley, November 2017).

avenues of legal asset protection. I've learned from past experience just how complicated it is to introduce an agreement late in the couple's married life.

Sophie was a second-generation inheritor of a large business, together with her three siblings. She had been happily married for 30 years, and one of her children was already married. When she and her siblings sat down to compose their Family Agreement, Sophie strongly felt that there should be no discrimination against spouses, while her siblings did not want shares to go to either their or their children's spouses. The discussion was carried out in a polite and respectful manner, but emotions were strong. At one point, Sophie even declared that she'd like to divorce her siblings, saying, "In my family, we believe in equality and unity. I am not going to force my children to have a prenup agreement." Sophie eventually agreed to a clause in the company documents that prevented shares from going to anyone other than direct descendants. She said that she did so only because her husband did not want the shares, and her children—who wanted to be part of the cousins' group—didn't want to stall the agreement.

Another case in point is that of the Ibrige family, who owned a medium-sized business, begun by three sons and their father. Their mother was employed elsewhere at the time but joined the family business when she retired. All the shares were in the hands of the parents, but profits were distributed among all five family members who ran the business. When the eldest son, who was also the CEO, was approaching his fiftieth birthday, he decided that he wanted to have his part of the shares in his name.

This wish triggered the Family Agreement creation process. The mother insisted that she would give up some of the shares, but only if they built in assurances that the shares she gave up would be protected from falling out of family hands. Discussions about all chapters of the agreement went smoothly. The partners decided quickly that third-generation family members would have to present a prenup agreement as a precondition for receiving company shares.

For the three brothers in the second generation, the issue was more complex. They had been married for more than twenty years; each couple had teenage children and planned to stay happily married. How could they ask their wives to sign an agreement now? The siblings were afraid to even raise the issue with their wives.

I took the task upon myself and held a conversation with each of the wives. It turned out that they did not oppose signing a written agreement that in the case of divorce, the private wealth (the house and money) would be split evenly, and that while the shares would remain in the husbands' hands, the wives would receive the value of their part in their husbands' shares. I went on to explain the logic behind it, assuring them that the shares would eventually go to their children. It seemed like an arrangement that everyone could agree to.

However, when the family's attorney discussed the practical implications of such an arrangement with the brothers, they backed off. They realized that in the case of divorce, and at the present value of the company, they would have to compensate their wives for their part of the shares, and this was a large amount of money—too much. Instead, they offered the wives an agreement under which in the case of divorce the wife would get a monthly allowance, and the shares would be kept for the children.

At this point, the wives took another attorney to represent them. Discussions continued, focusing on the allowance and the number of years it would be paid, and the discussions carried on for so long that the eldest brother's fiftieth birthday came and went. The Family Agreement was put aside, and the shares remained in the hands of the parents. Finally, I suggested that they sign a partial agreement, in order to have a set of rules for all other topics, hoping that the brothers stayed happily married so the issue of the shares never resurfaced. The brothers accepted the proposal and signed the partial agreement. They all felt that having an incomplete agreement was better than not having one at all.

PROCESSES

In the beginning of chapter 3, I described the ritual of the Seder. The rules for that ritual are well documented, but it is not the documentation that keeps the Seder alive throughout the generations; it is the process with which it is executed. Year after year, for more than three thousand years, on the same exact date, these rules come to life in every Jewish family's home. Process creates stability.

Families who decide to invest in continuity realize that this kind of investment is a marathon rather than a sprint. It's true that the first years are intense, as the family works on putting the policies and structures in place. But once this task is complete, it has to be put to use. The processes described in the written documents must be played out in the lives of the people for whom they are intended. And there are a lot of processes to put into action: an annual family meeting, a quarterly meeting of the Family Council, elections to the Family Council, educational programs for the next generation, written reports for board meetings, and meetings to review family member employment status, as specified in the Family Agreement. Naturally, engaging in socially responsible activities entails another set of processes that must occur. In addition, it is crucial to maintain contact with family members: to know the aspirations and endeavors of various family members, to listen to their grievances, and to hear those who may sometimes feel unheard.

These processes do not simply happen. Without an individual or committee to see to it that the system works, the system will *not* work. I've known families in which the mother had no official role, but she was the one who made it all happen. In rare cases, this role is made official. Many years ago, I heard a lecture by Philippe de Gaspé Beaubien II, from Montreal, Canada, in which he explained that while he was chairman of the board of their family business, his wife Nan-b was the head of the Family Council. They had decided that she would draw the same salary as the chairman of the board, although, as de Gaspé Beaubien put it, "her work was much harder than mine." Her task was to oversee the entire family system, to listen to everyone's wishes and complaints at all hours of the day, and to act sensitively but firmly to keep the system going.

In the Grambar family, the fourth-generation steering committee is in charge of keeping the system going. They prepare the yearly budget and present it to the Family Council for approval, they make the yearly schedule of all events (family meetings, Family Council meetings, fourth-generation educational events, etc.), and they monitor the execution of these events by the various governance bodies. The steering committee also developed a feedback system by which they could evaluate these activities and work on continuous improvement. They dedicate several hours every week to keeping the wheel turning. This is the kind of dedication to process that keeps a sprawling family business healthy.

CONCLUSION

To turn a family's vision of long-lasting continuity into reality, the family must anchor their insights and aspirations to real-world governing bodies, written documents, and consistently maintained processes. I like to think of it as a family's personal railroad. The governance entities can be thought of as railroad tracks laid on previously untraveled land. The rules defined in the Family Agreement are train carriages, which can carry the family system from its current state to its desired destination. And finally, there must be someone who makes the railroad system run, who sets the schedule and sees to it that the train leaves on time and reaches its destination consistently. Both the processes and the people who assume responsibility for them are essential to the family's journey.

CHAPTER 10

Family Agreements

When Moses ascended to the Heavenly heights, the ministering angels came before God, "Master of the Universe, what is someone born of a woman doing among us?"

God said to them, "He has come to receive the Torah."

Asked the angels, "You intend to give that to flesh and blood?"

God said to Moses, "Give them an answer."

And Moses said to God, "Master of the Universe, in the Torah that You are giving me, what is written?"

And God replied, "I am Your God Who has taken you out of the land of Egypt."

Moses turned to the angels, "Did you descend to Egypt? Were you enslaved by Pharaoh? Why should the Torah be yours? What else is written in it? 'Remember the Sabbath day to sanctify it.' Do you engage in any labor from which you would need to rest? What else is written in it? 'You shall not take the name of God in vain.' Are there any business transactions among you that might lead to oaths taken in vain? What else is written? 'Honor your father and mother.' Do you have a father or a mother? What else is written? 'You shall not murder; you shall not commit adultery; you shall not steal.' Is there envy among you? Is there evil inclination among you?"

Immediately the angels conceded to God.

R Yehoshua ben Levi, Talmud, Shabbat, 88b

When my family was young, we spent a lot of time with other young families. One afternoon, as my neighbor Sarah and I chatted on a park bench, her four-year-old son Michael ran past, covered in mud and waving a branch the full length of his body over his head. He was followed by my own young son, who was also armed with a stick. Sarah sighed, gave me an apologetic smile, and called her child over.

"Michael," she said, "We've talked about sticks. What did we say?"

Her boy looked at the ground and muttered sullenly, "Can't wave it over my head."

"That's right. This is the third time I've—"

Michael's mouth fell open, realizing consequences were upon him. Here he pointed to my son, "But HE—HE plays with sticks all the time!"

Sarah was unmoved. Deftly uncurling her son's fingers from his stick, she said, "I don't care. He's never hit his baby sister with a stick before, so he doesn't need this rule. But you have, so you do. Go sit."

Wailing, Michael retired to the roots of a nearby tree and sat out his punishment, and Sarah added the stick to the small pile at her feet.

Every family abides by its own set of rules, and those rules are borne out of the individual needs of each family member. Like the rules of our parents, designed to support our growth and shape us into responsible people, Family Agreements are about nurturing the overall family.

This isn't the sort of thing that can be done during a crisis—those moments where family members are in conflict or feel threatened are the absolute wrong time to try to impose rules that will bind the family for generations. But when the family lives in relative harmony, creating policies that will support individual members can head off most potential problems. This is especially important for family businesses because Family Agreements are designed to regulate the interactions among family members, specifically considering their wealth and their business operations.

Every Family Agreement bears the signature of the people who discussed its content, deliberated on it, and reached an agreement. The policies they established may be changed by future members or generations, but the basic model of having an agreement that establishes a set of rules and policies usually outlives the people who created it.

Because every family is different, Family Agreements are different from one another in format, content, and style. There is no part of a Family Agreement that is "standard," no part of it that is a template, no part that can be completed like a fill-in-the-blank form. But there are some basics.

When I work on a Family Agreement, I try to ensure that it covers the following topics.

THE BASICS

Values and Vision

I try to spend a considerable amount of time on the introduction to a family's document, knowing that it will set the tone for the rest of the document and inspire the family to really think about the values that guide their behavior. I want them to talk extensively about what they want their family to say to future generations. Some clients want to skip this section, convinced that their time must be focused on the policies and processes they are about to develop, but the truth is that at times, their inspirational legacy serves as a better protector of future family unity than the specific rules they have made.

Here are some examples of what different families wrote in their Family Agreements, in an effort to explain their thinking.

THE SMITH FAMILY

The members of the Smith Family have worked together closely and harmoniously since the founding of the company. Thanks to hard work and the relationship of mutual trust and respect shared by family members, the business has prospered and grown, and now, in view of the transfer of shares to the second generation, and at a time when the members of the third generation are reaching an age when they need to know the rules regarding employment in our company, we would like to formalize our rules of conduct in writing. We believe that the Family Agreement will contribute to maintaining the harmony and cooperation we share in the future as well.

The values that form the basis for the way we run the business and live and work together as a family are those that we were taught by our parents, the founders of the business. These values were, and continue to be, the solid foundation of our conduct.

- Professionalism
- Family cohesion
- Mutual respect (between the members of the family and toward our employees)
- Modesty
- Diligence
- Risk management

THE JONES FAMILY

1. We are a warm and loving family. As we aspire to maintain this close relationship in the future, we see a need to formulate shared rules and understandings to assure family harmony and the continuing prosperity of the business.

2. We consider active intergenerational partnership important—partnership in which our parents are an integral part of business and family life while the next generation develops the business, preserving the family legacy and the values of the founding generation.

3. We aspire to maintain a close relationship between our families, even if any of us live a physical distance away from the center of our business.

4. We aspire to "do good" both as a family and a firm. The agreements we have formulated will enable us to make decisions in this spirit and to ensure that they are implemented.

5. This pact was signed in the spirit of the agreement we reached. Nevertheless, we are aware that future changes and amendments in the spirit of the times are possible, and these will be made according to the procedures set forth in this pact.

6. The family relationship is the source of our strength. A history of conflicts in the extended family has taught us how important it is to work to achieve family harmony and refrain from repeating the past. We will always be here for each other regardless of the circumstances and will

maintain family unity in our business and social activities. To enable this connection, we aspire to maintain open, honest communication, and we will encourage feedback and accept criticism graciously.

7. Enjoyment. Taking pleasure in our work is one of the keys to our success and the uniqueness of our business. It is our desire to also cultivate joy and humor in our personal and family life and permit ourselves to enjoy the fruits of our labor.

8. Innovation and creativity. We aspire to be contemporary and innovative for the personal development and interest of each of us as well as to ensure added value for our customers. To this end we will make sure to persevere in learning, in keeping abreast of what is being done in our field in other countries, and in adopting new business directions and tools as necessary.

9. Excellence. We continually aspire to excellence. This requires innovation and renewal in all areas of our activity. Educated, experienced professionalism; personal diligence; and meticulous attention to quality are elements that have earned us a leading position in the market. We will preserve these elements and cultivate a reputation of excellence in every sphere in which we engage.

10. Contribution to society. We feel that contributing to the community in which we live is important, and we strongly believe in helping others and in good deeds and programs that deliver added value to society. We will seek out ways to realize this value in our professional and personal lives and in educating the succeeding generations of our family.

11. Economic well-being. We will work to ensure that the money will enable each of us to be independent and secure and will serve as a lever for the advancement of family members, our employees, and society.

THE WALLBERG FAMILY

Core Beliefs

a. As a family, we value loyalty and individuality. We treat one another as equals and act with fairness and compassion in mind.

b. We aspire that the family's wealth will last many generations and even grow over time. We intend to spend and make investments with this purpose in mind.

c. We want to discourage dissipation of wealth and recklessness, but rather to build and maintain a strong financial foundation that is informed by values. This should provide opportunities for many generations of family members to live productive, comfortable lives and contribute, in many and varied ways, to our communities.

d. Our goal is to ensure a reasonable standard of living for all family members, but not to encourage excessive distributions or spending. Receiving money that has not been earned directly should encourage, rather than impair, the individual's work ethic and our desire to contribute our time and wealth to charitable causes and institutions. Our hope is that family members of current and future generations may launch new endeavors, whether in business, charities, or other constructive pursuits. We encourage ambition but are cautious of unnecessary risk.

e. We embrace the responsibility of actively engaging in the management of the family's wealth. This includes being aware and informed of the workings of the family wealth structure and activities. We encourage and support family members to educate themselves in order to better manage the wealth and cultivate the outstanding professionals we entrust to assist us.

f. We hope that our family's success will foster both creative individuality and a profound commitment to the common good in future generations. It is our dream that they will possess the commitment and the adaptability to build on both the benefits our family has enjoyed and the values necessary to preserve them.

g. It is our hope that the family continues to manage the family wealth together because we believe that we are stronger together as investors and as a family unit. However, this may not be the next generation's desire and if after due discussion some or all of them wish to pursue their individual paths, we would wish that their objectives be accomplished in the smoothest way possible. In the end, the most important thing to us is that family harmony always be preserved.

These core beliefs were laid out by the founder and shared by the family, who were inspired by these beliefs and hopeful that future generations would be too. Core beliefs may be essential to the people who wrote them, and even inspirational to the generations that follow, but they are nonetheless open to review and adaptation by the family through the Family Council.

Ownership Structure

The Ownership Structure section opens the more "technical" part of the agreement. It specifies the current owners of the enterprise or wealth and the intended owners in the future. Sometimes the deliberations during work on this chapter constitute the first time that family members have spoken openly about sensitive issues, such as who will get what.

In the Hart family, for example, we discussed the Family Agreement with all the family members. The discussions dragged on for months, and it seemed that no progress was being made. Finally, the head of the family opened one of our meetings by saying, "I have finally reached a decision. I love you all dearly, but I do not wish to be your partner. Neither do I believe that you should be partners. Therefore, I shall continue to give you generous gifts. After my death, all my active businesses will be liquidated, and the proceeds will be split among you, as will be specified in our Family Agreement." Once the ownership issue was resolved, the rest of the Family Agreement was completed within a few weeks.

The Levin family came to me for help creating a Family Agreement. After interviewing each of them individually, it became clear that the "elephant in the room" was the question of who would take over ownership of the family business and other family assets. The family was a close and loving family, and no one wanted to hurt anyone's feelings. Even though the founder himself did not have a partner, he and his wife nevertheless believed that all three of their children would be future partners in everything.

Their unspoken expectations were deeply at odds with the reality of how they'd raised their children, who all had different ideas about the way they wanted to spend their lives. The challenge for this family was to openly discuss the pros and cons of future partnership and decide how ownership should be handled. They finally decided that the enterprise would go to the older brother, who had been actively managing it for the past fifteen years, while the others would each receive a share of the assets. Once that decision was reached, the rest was easy.

Governing Bodies

Does a family enterprise require a board of directors? When families sit down to discuss how they make decisions, it may be the first chance they've ever had to think deeply about how things really work in their family, and how processes could be improved.

When the third generation of the Gunderson family prepared their family's policy proposal, they initially decided that questions such as employment of family members and remunerations should be decided by the board of directors, while issues regarding next-generation preparation, family weekends, and gifts should be dealt with by the Family Council. However, they hit a stumbling block when they realized that there *was* no BOD in their family, and no Family Council. Their proposal to the senior generation suggested that such governing bodies be established immediately.

Rules of Engagement

"Who participates in what" is one of the most important questions for every family business. Often times, these burning issues focus on the following questions:

- Who is eligible to participate in each of the governing bodies?
- Can spouses work in the business?
- Can spouses receive shares?
- Who decides who sits on the BOD?
- Who is the Family Council comprised of?

The Question about whether shares can be transferred to spouses really asks whether shares can be transferred outside the family in case of the death or divorce of a shareholder. This is often a loaded and emotionally fraught issue. In order to "protect" the shares (i.e., keep them within the family), there should be a legal document or clause that transfers shares only to direct descendants and grants the spouse his or her *part of the value*, but not the shares themselves. The best-known way to do this is through either a prenuptial or postnuptial agreement (see chapter 9).

Exiting the Family Partnership

I believe that being a shareholder in a family business should not be a "life sentence." Successors need to be able to choose their own paths, and they need to know that doing so will not destroy their familial relationships or tear down everything they've worked to build. That's why I emphasize the value of including in the Family Agreement a carefully described procedure a shareholder should follow for divesting themselves of their shares. Even if no family member participating in the Agreement ever plans to sell their shares, the possibility should exist and must be spelled out.

For instance, John and Nick were equal partners in the family enterprise that their parents had founded. They were very close to each other, and their families practically lived together. Each of them owned a significant portion of the business, and selling even a small part seemed impossible. But three years after the Family Agreement had been signed, Nick announced that he wanted to sell his shares. Fortunately, the Family Agreement had already established the procedure for such an event: it stated that shares would be sold only to family members or to the company itself. The valuation mechanism was spelled out, together with the terms of payment. The siblings followed it to the letter, saving themselves a bitter fight. Not only did they not argue, they remained very close and continued to hold their private assets in a joint investment company. Their children, who were also shareholders, continued to be partners in the business.

Enjoying the Fruits

In many families, I've seen a certain amount of confusion over the various ways family members receive and use money. As an umbrella term, I like the phrase "enjoying the fruits" to refer to things like salaries, bonuses, gifts, dividends, and perks (cars, flights, expense budgets, etc.). But it is important to first distinguish among them, at least conceptually. For instance, if the father decides to give his son—who does not work in the family business—a monthly allowance, and he does it in the form of a salary, the son may get confused and believe that he earns a salary by merit, even though he doesn't contribute to the business. Even if, for tax benefits, this money is given through the business, it should be made clear to everyone involved that this is the son's allowance, not a salary.

Once these distinctions are made, the family can decide what should be given to whom, and whether it is given equally or according to need.

As I stressed earlier, each Family Agreement is unique, as it addresses the unique issues of a particular family. The Schultz Family Agreement is a case in point. It was created by the four second-generation siblings of the Schultz family business. In creating the Agreement, their main goal was to end the thirty-five-year-old system put in place by their father, the founder, who had arranged for the wealth of the family to belong to all family members "communally," meaning that there was no private wealth. This founder had spent some years in a kibbutz before starting his own business, and he admired the kibbutz's system of communal property, although he personally did not feel that it was right for him. Therefore, in the family he raised, everything belonged to everyone: the houses he bought for each of his children, the vintage car collection one of the spouses insisted on investing in … everything.

Each nuclear family used whatever it wanted, even though there were significant differences in lifestyle among the siblings. By the time the eldest of the third generation was old enough to go to college, the siblings of the second generation felt that the system had become a burden, and they wanted to do away with it. Here is how their Family Agreement reflected this effort:

Withdrawals from the Company and Offsetting Past Withdrawals and Purchases

THE SCHULTZ FAMILY

1. Commencing on _____, a record will be kept of withdrawals and/or purchases made by each of the shareholders of the company in such shareholder's credit and debit journal.

2. It is each shareholder's responsibility to report in writing on each of his withdrawals or purchases from the company's account by the end of the current quarter in which said withdrawals or purchases were made.

The parties shall make a financial reckoning once a year in respect of withdrawals or purchases made by any of the shareholders, which are not for the purpose of covering living expenses. Any dispute as to whether a particular expense should be included in living expenses will be unanimously decided by two of the siblings, and in the absence of agreement the expenditure shall not be included in living expenses.

3. At the beginning of each year, the board of directors will determine the salary payable to each of the holders of management shares who is employed by the company, as well as the maximum amount that a shareholder may withdraw from the company. The sum defined shall, on the one hand, reflect the needs of the shareholders' families so that they are able to live in financial comfort, and on the other, the financial position of the company on the basis of the prior year's performance. Any expenditure requested by a shareholder over and above these amounts shall be presented to the board of directors for approval before the expenditure or purchase is made.

4. Until the effective date that shall be defined, the financial reckoning between the shareholders with regard to withdrawals and purchases made by shareholders that do not constitute an expense or purchase or withdrawal or

payment for living expenses, shall be made up to such date as follows:

1. The value of the homes of each of the families shall be calculated according to its purchase value;

2. The value of real estate properties registered in the names of any of the shareholders shall be calculated in the same manner;

3. The funds deposited in savings, securities, and bank accounts shall be calculated according to their dollar value on the effective date;

4. The value of jewelry in the possession of any of the parties that was purchased with the company's funds shall be assessed according to its value on the effective date.

5. All other assets owned by the company and/or purchased with the company's funds, even if registered in the name of any of the parties, shall be offset on the date of dissolution or retirement of any of the shareholders of the company.

6. Funds remaining to the credit of any of the shareholders after the above reckoning and offset shall remain to the credit of said shareholder, and they shall be entitled to withdraw the sum owed to their credit from the company immediately if they are in need of said funds. To the extent that the need for the funds is not urgent, they shall be entitled to withdraw the funds from the company according to the company's financial position and its needs.

Rules of Employment for Family Members

Considering that so much of a Family Agreement is built around protecting the family business as it presses on into the future, it can be no surprise that the Agreement must concern itself with providing rules and clarity for the successors who have yet to join the business, especially because the path to employment within the family business is often a rocky one.

The principle that guides most families when they work on rules of employment is that they have to *protect the business from the family, and the family from the business*. This means that the business needs employees who are well-trained, well-educated, and suitable for the specific jobs. Michael Strauss always pointed out to his family that the business is the cow that gives the milk the entire family drinks, and it is therefore the task of the family to make sure that the cow gets the best of everything: the best cowshed, the best food, the best veterinary care, and the best caretaker. Only in this way can the cow give the best and most nutritious milk. Therefore, family members would be employed only if they met all the requirements of any given job.

Most of the families I work with decide in advance that the Family Agreement will not attempt to change the employment status quo, as inadequate as it may be. Rather, they wish to avoid repeating the mistakes of the past in the next generation's employment prospects.

Another element that might be emotionally loaded for family members is the issue of who determines salaries, bonuses, and perks for employed family members. When in the hand of the patriarch, these decisions tend to be emotionally driven rather than merit-driven. The lack of transparency throughout the issue gives rise to jealousy, frustrations, and animosity. Therefore, in many cases, the decision that salaries and bonuses must be decided by the BOD, not by an individual family member, plays the biggest role in alleviating tension and frustration among family members.

Here is how the Gunderson family defined their rules of employment:

THE GUNDERSON FAMILY

Guidelines

1. We recognize that each one of us is seeking the right place for themselves on the axis between focus on the individual (their own self-actualization and that of their nuclear family) and belonging to the larger family (loyalty to the family legacy, belonging to a branch of the family).

2. We wish to preserve the family ties between the members of the family, regardless of whether or not they choose to be part of the circle of joint ownership and management.

3. We believe that the key to healthy intergenerational continuity lies in cultivating the extended family as taking priority over the historical interests of a particular branch of the family, which had existed within the family.

4. The family attributes importance to the managerial involvement of family members in the companies it owns.

5. We wish to create a situation in which family members have an interest in involving the family's assets in their business activities. In this way, we can enlist the entrepreneurship and professionalism of family members for the benefit of

the assets of the entire family, without detriment to their motivation.

6. The principle of professionalism is of paramount importance, as it maximizes shareholder value. The employment of executives who are family members will be based on the principle of professionalism and suitability for the job.

Employment rules:

a. The rules refer to the founders' direct descendants and their partners/spouses.

b. Family members may fill managerial positions as well as senior professional positions that do not include a managerial component (e.g., chief technologist).

c. A family member may not be permanently employed in a junior position unless they are a candidate for promotion to the senior position of CEO/VP in an organization that has several vice presidents, or to a senior professional position that reports to the CEO.

d. Additionally, any family member who is interested may pursue an internship in the company in a non-management position, for a period of no more than two years. Beyond said period, the rules above shall apply.

e. Family members are invited to join the company in a management training track. On joining, a management training track will be planned for them. The first job will be as per the required qualifications and according to the company's needs and will be considered an apprenticeship. The board of directors' employment and remuneration committee will define the trainee's accompaniment in this period and the amount of their salary as a trainee.

f. A family member may be a salaried employee or an entrepreneur but may not be both at the same time.

g. The board of directors' employment and remuneration committee shall be responsible for the job definition, for measurement of the family member's performance, and for recommendations for their promotion/termination of employment.

h. The committee's recommendations will require the agreement of the employer company's CEO and the approval of the board of directors of the family holding company.

Incapacitation

Discussing the sensitive topic of "What happens if..." is difficult. This is particularly true among second-generation family members, the children of founders who are the unquestionable leaders of their extended family. Lansberg (1988) describes this difficulty as the "succession conspiracy," suggesting that it is the failure to adequately plan for the inevitable that leads to the decline of family businesses after the loss of the founder.[14] It is far better to discuss the "What happens if..." questions when everything is peaceful and everybody is healthy. Clear-headed consideration of these questions enables the family to plan for emergency cases, so that in times of emotional stress, when

---

14   Ivan Lansberg, "The Succession Conspiracy," *Family Business Review* 1, no. 2 (June 1988): 119–143.

the real need arises, they can rely on a preestablished set of rules. Moreover, thinking about these questions can be a maturing experience in and of itself, in that it requires family members to deal with such a sensitive issue and reach a practical decision.

The following excerpt is taken from an agreement made between two unrelated partners who built a successful company together. Although they were not blood-related, their company and families grew together, and they felt a strong bond between them. But no matter how strong that bond was, they knew that if something happened to either of them, they had to let the families be independent.

THE LAUREL COMPANY

Incapacitation: General

a. In a case of incapacitation of a partner, it is essential to maintain the continued existence of the company until a decision with regard to the future has been made. Therefore, the remaining partner will continue to manage the company fully, with minimum disruption by the representatives of the incapacitated partner.

b. The incapacitation agreement is made between the partners as Joint CEOs of the company and as members of the board of directors of the company.

c. In a case of gradual deterioration in the mental or physical condition of a partner, the second partner, together with the first partner's wife, shall decide on a competency evaluation by an appropriate physician. The first partner's wife shall be responsible for the performance of the evaluation. The results of this assessment shall be binding.

Management of the company in case of incapacitation

a. In the event of the inability to continue working in the company temporarily or for an unknown period, the remaining partner will assume the incapacitated partner's responsibilities and will make decisions on his own.

b. After six months' incapacitation for medical reasons, the remaining partner shall consult the incapacitated partner's wife. One of the options set forth in a clause below, shall be declared by them consensually.

c. The partner who is incapacitated for medical reasons shall continue to receive a salary and the financing of all medical treatments over and above those covered by medical insurance, until the dissolution of the partnership.

d. In the event of death, the family shall be paid the deceased's salary until the dissolution of the partnership.

e. If the company becomes a public company, the company will be managed according to the rules applying to the conduct of public companies.

Ownership in circumstances of incapacitation

a. In circumstances of incapacitation, the remaining partner may choose one of four options:

　　i. Acquisition of the incapacitated partner's holding according to terms and conditions that shall be consensually decided together with the incapacitated partner's wife.

　　ii. Sale of the entire company to a third party.

iii. A [Buy Me Buy You] BMBY transaction with the incapacitated partner's family.

iv. Acceptance of the incapacitated partner's wife as partner. In such case, she will be granted full rights in the management of the company and on the board of directors.

Philanthropy

All the families I work with seem to give considerable amounts of money to causes they feel will advance the social welfare of the world at large, though that giving is often only at the initiative of one family member (usually the head of the enterprise). In many cases the rest of the family learns about it only when they receive an award or some kind of external recognition. My conversations with families convey the message that the portion of the family wealth dedicated to social responsibility can and should be:

a. Strategically planned, so as to ensure that the family gives to a cause that is meaningful to them.

b. Executed as a joint family affair, thus strengthening family ties around a positive common cause.

The younger generation is generally very interested in social responsibility. Many successors are concerned that the family's money may have been made in ways that did harm (to the environment, to the labor force, etc.), and they want to ensure that their businesses, at least, do no harm. Indeed, they often actively seek to do actual good.

Conversations centered around making the world a better place usually lead to the details of impact investing and other financial tools that currently exist, on the spectrum between "sheer business" and traditional charity. Young successors understand that in order to achieve a transformation from the old way of doing business to a socially responsible way, they should engage the entire family in making it happen. Giving can no longer be a one-man show, performed far from the eyes of family members.

When a family is ready to transform its philanthropic giving into a strategic socially responsible activity, it welcomes the opportunity to incorporate it into their Family Agreement. In these cases, families usually specify a field in which they want to be involved (education, health, ecology, etc.), and they determine which family governance body will be in charge of execution and communication with the rest of the family.

The Praegar family established a charitable foundation and then did considerable work on creating their strategy for the foundation. In their Family Agreement, though, this was mentioned only once: in the outline of Governing Bodies, they stated that the Family Council "serves as the supervising body for the philanthropic activities of the Family, makes decisions regarding significant philanthropic gifts made by the Family, and allocates responsibility for dealing with each philanthropic activity."

Changing and Updating the Family Agreement

Although the Family Agreement is intended for the current and future generations of the family, most families understand that the Agreement must be a living document, something that can be updated according to circumstances. Therefore, the last chapter in every Agreement specifies the procedure for updating the Agreement. Here is how one family decided to do it.

THE ABBOT FAMILY

1. The Agreement will be reviewed by the Family Council once every two years. The review will be initiated by the Family Council Secretary.

2. In the first two years after the completion of the Agreement, it will not be changed except by unanimous decision of the Family Council. Thereafter, any Family Council member can present a suggestion for a change or update, at any time.

3. The suggestion should be handed in writing to the secretary, who will include it in the agenda of the upcoming Family Council meeting.

CONCLUSION

The excerpts from Family Agreements displayed in this chapter were not meant to be copied. They are exhibited here to show how similar issues may result in very different policies. Each family addresses its own unique situation.

CHAPTER 11

How Is It Done?

A prisoner can't free himself from prison.

Talmud Bavli Baba Metzia, 30b

People have an enormous capacity to change their life through sheer will and self-discipline, but we can't do *everything* by ourselves. We get stuck on things, sometimes small and silly, sometimes huge and overwhelming, and we need another person to help us get past them, just like handcuffs must be cut off by someone else. Once freed of those handcuffs, the prisoner can do the rest on their own. This is how I think of my work at Dorot—I am that someone else. Many of the family members I work with are imprisoned; imprisoned by their perceptions, by parental expectations, by the circumstances of being "paper rich, cash poor," or by the habits and patterns set by their family history. My work gives them a process that lets them escape that claustrophobic mind-set. I open the gate to new options. To a life of personal choice, of transparency, of growth and innovation. A future that is entirely theirs to build.

It sounds great, right? But how does it happen? That's the first question I hear from clients after I speak about succession and continuity: "How is it really done?" How can an outsider change the way things have been done in their family for years, or generations? How can they control the way their wealth affects their lives, rather than letting it wreak havoc on their career paths and family relations? This chapter is about exploring that *how*. It's about the journey we take from now to the moment wealth becomes a platform for personal development and enhanced family relations.

KICK-STARTING

We've already talked about the conversations that need to take place, the personal choices people have to make, the working partnerships that should be created, and the written documents that should anchor it all. Still, making it all happen can seem achingly out of reach.

For many families, kick-starting the project is the hardest part of the journey. Take, for example, the Ellison siblings, who contacted me after hearing my Family Business Continuity lecture. I had a meeting with the four of them and gave them a written proposal for a Family Agreement. Upon reading it, they stuttered and stalled, and eventually stopped returning my calls. I understood. It's one thing for you to be sure of the need to change, but it's another to convince everyone else. Eleven years later, the siblings returned and presented me with the original proposal I had written for them. It had taken them some time, but they were now ready to begin.

In Amy's family, the kick-start point is still far ahead. Amy, a fifth-generation member of a two-branch family, wanted to create a "school of ownership" for her peers in the fifth generation, with whom she'd already collaborated a fair amount; she wasn't trying to change the way the fourth generation operated. But when she brought her plan to the fourth-generation chairman of the board and requested a budget, she was bluntly turned down. "This doesn't make any sense," her uncle said. "I shall not have it."

Amy was devastated. What she hadn't considered was the possibility that her uncle felt threatened by the project. She hadn't anticipated the ways her program might affect the rest of the family, so she hadn't seen the value in obtaining their buy-in beforehand. Eventually she realized that she would have to allay her uncle's fears before she could get the program going and kick-start a much larger journey for her family.

The first issue to be addressed—whether it's adopting a Family Agreement, enacting a preparation program for the next generation, or establishing a board of directors—is usually the concern that burns hottest in the minds of people who know that something must be done, but who either aren't sure what it is or can't seem to get their families to buy into it. These people are usually successors, and over the years, I've seen them tackle this problem through several different strategies.

Giving Information

This is the most rational approach, one in which the successor shares information with their seniors about the ways other families have succeeded in keeping the enterprise and family together for generations. For most successors, that information comes from an article they've read, a recent study, or a lecture they've just attended. But successors don't necessarily need to cite information about other families. In some ways, relying on the senior generation's imagination can be even more powerful.

In a private conversation with one such successor, Professor Ivan Lansberg suggests appealing to the senior generation's own powers of deduction. He suggests presenting the senior with a timeline: "Just think about it, Dad. In twenty years, you'll probably retire [assuming that the founder is around sixty-five, the prospect isn't that frightening]. By the time you do, your successors will need to have spent around ten years learning to run the enterprise. We'll need five years before that to become truly helpful to you, which means that even before then, we'll need five years to learn to communicate amongst ourselves and become a team. Altogether, that's twenty years of work before we can be the effective, prosperous successors that you want us to be. That means we need to start now."

The exact length of time needed will vary for individual families with different skill sets, but the important thing is to convince the senior that work must begin immediately, and they must play an active part in that work, or at least give their permission for the work to begin.

Rational appeals don't work on everyone; so, if this approach fails, successors may try another tack.

The Mother-Bear Model

When she talks about successors kick-starting a process, my colleague, Tal Yahav, likes to use the analogy of the mother bear and her cubs. A mother bear is responsible for protecting and feeding her cubs and for teaching them the skills and knowledge to someday pursue a life without her. Apart from fulfilling those responsibilities, the mother bear isn't really all that interested in what her cubs get up to. She has her own life to live, and she doesn't want to be disturbed; so, as long as they don't bug her too much, her cubs can do whatever they want with themselves. Our clients, the Grambars, were taking the *cub* role when they established their fourth-generation education program. Promising that it wouldn't involve the seniors in any way, they presented the rationale and plan to their senior generation and requested a budget. It was only when they invited them to hear what they'd spent the past year doing that the parents became interested.

Mother bear decided—entirely on her own—that she wanted to get involved!

One Mountain at a Time

The Gundersons knew that their seniors were practical people. They might agree to addressing a "practical" issue, such as employment or remunerations, but they weren't about to involve themselves in a wide-open continuity process that could last years and eat up all their spare time. Knowing the challenge before them, the junior Gundersons decided to focus on one concrete issue: remunerations for work done by third-generation members for the benefit of the enterprise and/or the family. The task was relatively small but could potentially be expanded if the family received it well. In keeping with the small scope of the project, the junior Gundersons decided that the outcome of their work would be a proposal that they would present to their seniors, meaning that the decision to implement any of the proposed changes would rest entirely in the hands of the seniors. Rather than committing to an entire "journey," the junior Gundersons focused on climbing the mountain that stood in front of them. Once they overcame that hurdle, they could reevaluate the situation and go on to the next issue.

Quality Time

Spending "quality time" with an adult son or daughter is a rare treat for many parents (especially if their child is a dynamic, young career person), and it can have a profound effect on the relationship between them. Particularly if the time spent together is in a new setting—in which both parties can exhibit traits and proficiencies that might have otherwise gone unseen in their more familiar surroundings—parents and children can come to see each other in a new light and perhaps gain a deeper understanding of each other's motivations and foundational requirements. I have seen members of the junior generation invite their father or mother to spend a week with them at a family business seminar (at Kellogg, Harvard, IMD, or others), and once the senior came to see their child in this new, professional arena, and participated in the succession conversations going on all around them, they were persuaded to do something to ease the succession process within their own family enterprise.

A Tiny Toll

Eva graduated from law school and decided that she would join the retail business her mother had founded. The mother was naturally thrilled: for years she had wished that her daughter would join her, but she had been afraid to suggest it. When Eva presented her condition for joining—a meeting with a family business consultant, and a formal agreement drawn up between the two of them—it sounded to her mother like a small price to pay for her daughter's involvement in the business. In retrospect, Eva's mother saw that clarifying expectations and setting rules had been crucial to Eva's successful integration into the business.

Apparent Tension and Dissatisfaction

Preventative intervention is usually the wisest path, but it is not always possible. There are families in which one must wait to resolve issues—sometimes for years—until dissatisfaction and tension have broken the façade of family calm and revealed the longstanding needs beneath. For Mark, this moment arrived when he closed a deal on his most successful development project, and a large sum of money appeared on the horizon. Jealousy began to appear among his children, and they grew angry at Mark for his perceived fatherly sins.

In Mark's words, "I began to feel that my success was not a blessing, and that the money I'd receive would be cursed." It wasn't until Mark saw the disastrous effects of longstanding (previously invisible) patterns of control that he saw a need to act.

The Ultimatum

Bill and Aron were siblings and second-generation successors of a family enterprise. Bill was responsible for most of the business successes, and he was very close to his brother, whom he felt he needed by his side in order to succeed. Moreover, their parents had wanted them to stick together; they said their legacy was represented in Bill and Aron's partnership. But after a series of difficult conflicts between the two men, Aron informed his brother that he'd decided to leave the enterprise. Bill was devastated. He asked Aron, "What would it take to make you stay?" Aron took a few days to think about it and then gave Bill his ultimatum: "Start a continuity-planning process." The ultimatum worked. The family embarked on a process that has continued into the third and fourth generations. A word of warning: empty threats can do more harm than good. Unless you're genuinely willing to follow through, this method can actually worsen the situation.

When All Else Fails

Sometimes, none of these strategies work out. The transition from first to second generation is the most difficult, and it is the stage at which we see the highest rate of failure. There are founders who are simply unwilling to undertake any deliberations, or even to have a serious conversation with their successors. There are a number of reasons for this seeming intransigence:

1. **The Pharaohs' Syndrome.** When the pharaohs of ancient Egypt passed away, they had their vast wealth buried with them. Some founders, like those ancient pharaohs, have an unconscious wish to see the empires they've built vanish with them. This phenomenon seems to contradict the natural instinct for continuity and can usually be detected only in retrospect. A friend of mine, a self-described "survivor" of a family business, told me that his father's business, the one he'd built from the ground up, was sold for scraps four years after his death. The successors had been fighting with one another, and all were penniless. My friend commented that his father would probably have been reassured to know that he was the only person in the family talented enough to be capable of running such a business. All others—including his sons and grandsons—had failed.

2. **Queen Elizabeth's Attitude.** It sounds harsh, but some founders are uninterested in taking into account the needs and interests of other people. They've done so much work on their own that they feel they can safely ignore the opinions of everyone around them. Rachel and Miriam had worked together in their father's enterprise since high school, and neither of them knew anything else. When their children became teenagers, the two sisters realized that they needed clarity regarding their future employment status and ownership. They asked their parents to work together on a Family Agreement, but the parents refused. They were even turned down when they requested a raise in salary and bonuses, despite their feeling that between the two of them, they were carrying the burden of the

entire business. When asked why, their mother replied, "You are employees. If you don't like it, you can always seek a job somewhere else. I can carry on with external managers." Both sides knew that the sisters had no outside qualifications, and neither sister could possibly match the economic comfort they had by keeping the status quo. They were trapped. So, Rachel and Miriam stayed on in the business, waiting silently for their parents' old age.

3. **Emotional Anxiety.** Founders are mighty doers. They are industrious, driven, and ambitious. Often, however, they are not great talkers. They spend their best years solving problems and striking deals, away from their families and remote from the emotional ups and downs of their children. When those children become adults and the founders grow old, they are still unable to face the emotional demands in front of them. Moreover, they feel unsure of the shaky parent-child relationships that they *have* built and are therefore afraid that if they engage in an open conversation with their successors, they may lose the control they currently hold (through money). So, lacking better tools for handling family relations, they choose not to enter any discussion of the changing circumstances. This gives them the false sense that they are in control and will continue to be in control forever.

SETTING GOALS

Once the consent of the family is obtained, I can move to the next phase, that of setting the goals for the journey. Years ago, I attended a Family Business International Seminar, where I met an executive who had built his career by being the first external CEO for a series of family-owned businesses. Owners would bring him in, asking him to create order out of their chaos, but once he began to make an impact, they'd discover that they couldn't handle the changes he was making. They would invariably threaten to fire him. After years of this drama—which was as traumatic for him as it was for the owners—he learned to walk a narrow path by introducing change incrementally, and always keeping it at a pace that the owners could tolerate.

Setting goals for a continuity process is similarly challenging. I listen to the wishes of the family and then put the goals in writing—making them somewhat more ambitious than what the family had initially requested, but not too remote. Experience has taught me that change lies just beyond what we think we can achieve, but I still try to remember that I cannot "fix the family." True change comes from internal motivation, not from the goals I set, so I've found that my challenge is to define goals that will encourage the family to make the desired transition, without asking them to do anything that is truly beyond their abilities, or their will.

Here are some examples of the wishes of clients when they first met with me and the goals I set in the written proposal:

	FAMILY WISHES	GOALS DEFINED IN THE WRITTEN PROPOSAL
FAMILY A	Find an appropriate job for the eldest successor, enabling him to learn the business and preparing himself to take over for his father.	1. Career counseling for the eldest son, so as to determine the best career path for him (inside or outside the family business), in view of eventual continuity. 2. Open a family dialogue regarding future ownership and rules of employment for all siblings. 3. Plan the parents' giving strategy. 4. For the future, establish an ownership education program for the siblings.
FAMILY B	Help third-generation members introduce changes that will improve ownership control and resolve tension among branches.	1. Team building for third-generation members who are on the BOD. 2. Prepare a Family Agreement. 3. Plan ownership transition from second to third generations. 4. Strengthen BOD by adding external board members.
FAMILY C	Maintain current solidarity and warm relations among all family members, in consideration of initial signs of tension among siblings.	1. Plan parents' giving to their children, after hearing children's wishes. 2. Construct a Family Agreement through joint family discussions. 3. Create an ownership education program for siblings (either as a group or individually). 4. Work through a structured program dedicated to creating a working partnership.

FAMILY D	Stop fighting among siblings.	1. Define the career and development track for each of the siblings working in the family business, in conjunction with the parents' gradual release of management roles/responsibilities.
		2. Turn the siblings into a team of future owners.
		3. Establish a Family Agreement.

Not all the goals will be implemented. As often happens in a journey, unexpected needs emerge and new hurdles appear. The way forward is constantly being evaluated and reevaluated in light of changing circumstances, new possibilities, and the changing desires of family members. In this initial phase of the process, defining these goals primarily serves to create a vision of the future, of the kind of transformation that is necessary and possible. Setting these goals gives the initial wish a chance to materialize.

It's at this point that I suggest a family gathering, to present myself and the project we are about to begin. To give the gathering a warm, family atmosphere, I try to host it at the parents' home, in the evening hours, with everyone (including spouses) present. Hugs, laughter, and favorite dishes all communicate celebration, rather than an arduous undertaking, which makes it easy to coordinate individual meetings (the raw material for the "map" of the family and enterprise). Once the family is happily on board, we can move on to the next stage.

CREATING AN ACCURATE MAP

The Venn diagram in chapter 5 cannot possibly illustrate the extent to which the family enterprise is a multilayered system made up of individuals, each of them with their own strengths, weaknesses, aspirations, achievements, and disappointments. Every individual has a history, a present, and a dream of their desired future. I have always been fascinated by the life stories of the founders, but there are perspectives that easily get overlooked: the wife of the son, the middle daughter who holds a relatively insignificant job in the enterprise (but is always there), or the uncle who left the family business grudgingly many years ago and hasn't spoken with the father ever since. I wouldn't dare begin the process—to start down this long road—without meeting each person individually (those I can get hold of), listening to their stories, and establishing trust and personal rapport.

My knowledge of and relationships with these individuals creates the map I use to navigate the rocky terrain of long-term growth and development within families. I like to think of my initial meetings with individual family members as an opportunity for them to add a little more detail to my map, as though with each conversation, more ink appears on my parchment—here a hidden sinkhole, there an unexpected vista. As my map grows in detail, I become better able to chart the family's path to success.

A word about spouses: I am often asked (skeptically), why I need to meet the spouses. "They aren't participating in the process anyway," is what I am often told. There are two reasons for my wanting to meet with them in this initial phase:

    a. By explaining the process to the spouse, I can rely on their support behind the scenes, rather than having to compensate for their suspicion.

b. Spouses see the family with a unique perspective. Members of the family are so used to certain patterns of behavior that they often don't see those patterns as being specific to their family, so the external-internal view of the spouse can be incredibly valuable.

The complete map creates clarity and transparency. It acknowledges both the strengths and the difficulties that confront the family. Family members don't always tell one another what they really think, usually out of fear that this knowledge might prove explosive—and disastrous to the whole family. I've found that in the presence of a third party (either me or my colleagues), the family has the space to safely absorb difficult information. Once the whole map is presented, everyone is on the same page. From there, getting to work is relatively straight forward.

THE ROLE OF THE TOUR GUIDE

My role at this point, is that of a guide. There are lots of ways for a family to reach their chosen destination, and because I've made this journey many times, I can present the pros and cons of each path. It may take us through a retreat for the successors, or a series of two- to three-hour meetings, or intergenerational dialogues, or planning sessions for seniors only. However it goes, I can alert everyone to potential pitfalls along the way, and when someone slips, I can help them climb back up. I've seen how other families have handled myriad different problems, and I can always suggest solutions. But each journey is unique.

Ultimately, I can only show them the path. It is the family who must walk it.

HOW LONG DOES IT TAKE?

The mapping phase is usually easy to plan in advance, and the length of time required for it depends on the number of people to be interviewed and the time it takes to piece the map together and present it to the family.

The journey itself is harder to predict. It can depend on personalities, travel engagements, and priorities. I've seen it stretch anywhere from ten months to several years, though around a year is reasonably typical. Change does not happen overnight, and in some cases, multiple stages of incremental change are necessary—to avoid what my CEO friend calls "alteration shock."

But the process cannot drag on indefinitely. Change consumes a lot of energy and is tiring, and constant deliberation will just result in the family growing frustrated and angry. It is best if the family works through the process, completes it, and moves on to something else.

A PAIR OF CONSULTANTS

Whenever possible, I prefer to work with another experienced consultant. I have two such colleagues, and I try to have one of them involved in any of my projects. There are several reasons for this. The first is that four eyes and four ears are better than two. Whenever there is a meeting with more than one person, there are multiple voices, feelings, and coalitions in the room. Four eyes and ears can take it all in exponentially better than two can. This is especially true whenever the consultant has to facilitate the discussion and also listen and see everything. Whenever I have the privilege of facilitating the discussion with a colleague acting as a witness for the process, I inevitably discover that they noticed things I missed.

Moreover, individuals develop different rapports with different people. The younger daughter may feel quite comfortable talking to my colleague, but mesh badly with me—or vice versa. I want everyone to feel close and safe with me, but people are different, and that doesn't always happen. With two consultants in the room, a family member can take her pick. She can identify with whomever makes her feel the most comfortable. This means that the family has a better experience, and we get a clearer view of the situation, enabling us to better guide the family.

Finally, working with a colleague allows me to model teamwork, partnership, and mutual respect for the benefit of the family. Many clients have told me that, in retrospect, watching me work with a colleague has given them an example of how one can trust a teammate—how it is possible to think together, healthily voice differences, and still rely on each other. Since teamwork and partnership are often challenging for successors, it is important for them to see that it works, day in and day out.

WORKING WITH OTHER PROFESSIONALS

Having a systemic approach helps me diagnose the needs of subsystems and individual members, within both the family and the enterprise. It does not mean that I am equipped to provide all types of assistance. I know only too well what I do not know: legal issues, financial problems, tax issues, business strategy, family therapy, individual therapy, and philanthropic activities, among doubtless many other disciplines, are not my areas of expertise. To meet all the family's needs, I collaborate with other professionals. Sometimes, these are people who are already working with the family, but if it's necessary, I can introduce the family to other professionals, and they can choose someone who suits them.

INTERNATIONAL COLLABORATIONS

There are any number of reasons for families to scatter their descendants across the globe, whether it's for the sake of asset diversification or simply to maintain a global presence. In other cases, the dispersion happens as a result of personal choices made by individuals. But governance and management still require shared vision and values, which means that my role, and that of my colleagues, is to assist the family in developing a coordinated plan that can work even for its furthest-flung members. This inevitably requires collaboration with professional colleagues all over the world.[15]

While advancements in technology have rendered communication far simpler than in days past, geography-related considerations should not be overlooked. Living and working in a certain place means adopting a culture and a way of communicating that are specific to a given location. Having a consultant in the same geographic location as part of the family enables us to offer learning opportunities unique to that particular location. However, even more important is the ability for us all to better understand our conversations with family members, which might be misinterpreted by a consultant who was not exposed to the particular culture of the family. This collaboration encompasses more than simply overcoming geographical boundaries via video conferencing, etc. The real added value that each consultant brings is the deep cultural understanding and grasp of local resources that are often needed in this process.

---

15 Judith Peck and Tamar Milo, "International Collaboration between Consultants and Family," *International Family Offices Journal* (September 2017).

TRANSPARENCY

Management in today's world has become flat and transparent, but many family patriarchs still try to rule by secrets and manipulation. I often wonder how it can be that people know what goes on in the Oval Office within minutes of an event but continue to believe that they can keep secrets within their own families. When I start working with a family, I introduce a model of transparency in which emails are sent to everyone involved and participants agree on what should be reported from every meeting. It is a powerful model that breaks the circle of hidden agendas, manipulative secrets, and negative assumptions.

FOLLOW-UP

As I mentioned before, a project typically lasts about a year. I'm not interested in being a crutch for the whole family to lean on—my aim is to give family members the tools they need to continue on their own. Knowing that once the process is over they will return to their busy lives, some families decide to have a follow-up meeting once a year. Others decide to review the Family Agreement once every few years, while still others agree that the consultant will be the final authority in conflict resolution. Whatever the family decides, a follow-up mechanism helps realign the family toward the resolutions and achievements they have made and keeps the impact of the intervention alive.

CONCLUSION

Sometimes we need someone else to kick-start a process, and once it is started, we can continue on our own. This is what I do for families—I empower them to begin a journey.

It gives me great satisfaction to hear from new clients that their model is a family I worked with years ago. My new clients don't know that their role models received initial assistance from a professional, and they don't need to know. But for me, it is everything I work for. My greatest pride is knowing that a family accepted help, and that they used the tools I gave them to construct a future far happier and with fewer frustrations than they could ever have hoped for.

And then, there are the individuals I've touched along the way, the ones whose lives were transformed because of a difficult decision I helped them to make. One received the mandate to run the family business, with the blessing of the seniors and his Gen Peers. Another dared to leave the family business, get an MBA, and embark on an independent career. Yet another formed a partnership with the sibling she'd spent years competing against. Knowing that I touched people and helped them make their lives better is the greatest satisfaction I can ask for.

Families are beautiful, resilient entities, capable of feats of extreme kindness and cohesion and generosity. I am truly privileged to have spent my career working with them.

CHAPTER 12

Should We Talk?

Death and life are in the hand of the tongue, and those who love it will eat its produce.

Proverbs, 18:21

I wrote this book for the next generation in family enterprises. My aim was to give successors inspiration, ideas, and tools to leverage their unique situation for the benefit of themselves, their families, and society. Given that the inner workings of a family business are deeply complex, and often hard to fully understand from within the family, this book attempts to give a road map for successful continuity.

Built on a web of relationships, family businesses require empathy and communication to endure the passage of time and to embrace the innovation that must come with each generation. Without those two necessities, individual family members—and successors in particular—can find themselves feeling isolated and powerless.

The challenges that successors face are distinct from those of other young adults, whose families don't share a company. As a professional who has worked with family enterprises for more than two decades, I see those challenges over and over again. As a successor, you may feel like the weight of the world is on your shoulders, and no one else could ever possibly understand.

But it doesn't have to be that way. I'm here to tell you that isn't true. Scores of other successors have stood where you're standing now. There is wisdom to be gained by reaching out and connecting with people who can help.

Remember Lucas, whose uncle runs the family business? He felt like he'd never be able to advance because his uncle would always favor his cousins. Since his uncle will always be in charge of the business, there's nothing Lucas can do. His uncle's behavior wasn't going to change on its own, and with no apparent way to change the situation, Lucas's only hope was to look outside of the system. I helped him explore the possibilities that existed outside of his working environment. We looked for cousins who felt the same way. We looked for other family members who wanted transparency and to set rules for remuneration and advancement. Above all, we put him in touch with his Gen Peers, his partners for change. By discussing his options with an external professional, and seeing how it worked in other family businesses, Lucas was able to push for change from within.

Sometimes, all it takes is a sympathetic ear and a little perspective. Nadia's problem—the feeling that her sacrifice for the good of the company would go unnoticed and unrewarded in the name of equality—was rooted in a deeply jumbled mind-set. Whenever she thought about the future, she was overwhelmed—by the fear that change might damage her financial security; by the confusing blur between work and ownership; by the fantasy that some day things would just magically be better; and by a discomfiting resentment of her incompetent cousins. It was mental spaghetti, and she couldn't think straight. But during a conversation with a professional versed in these issues, she found herself able to objectively describe her concerns and judge the value of her various options. With a clear mind, she was able to make a decision and shift from passive frustration to proactive planning.

Having the courage to say aloud the things you really want can work wonders—particularly if you're saying those things to someone who wants, above all else, to see you and your family business bloom. Ken felt sure that he wanted to do something else. He was passionate about cooking, and he felt like that passion was being crushed by the work he did for his family's company. But when he sat down with us, he realized that he'd never really considered taking his passion for cooking beyond his own kitchen. Did he really see himself as a professional chef? Would he enjoy that lifestyle? The financial security that came with working for the family business was a serious consideration—could he really see himself living outside that bubble? When he sat down with us, we helped him to chart out the pros and cons of switching careers, and we recommended that he take a personal strengths test and deeply consider the results.

Above all, we validated his feeling of dissatisfaction but took pains to emphasize that in his pursuit of empowered choice, he has many different options. Whatever he chooses to spend his life doing, he'll choose it with clear eyes and a level head, which will go a long way toward building a fulfilling life.

But sometimes it's not enough to just choose our own path. Many of the millennials I've worked with have a very clear vision of the way they want to influence the future of their families' companies, but they're bogged down by the hesitancy of the senior generation.

Fiona, for instance, found herself dissatisfied with how slowly her company was adapting to the innovation required by the market and the constantly changing world. Like many millennials, Fiona was more interested in fast growth through acquisitions or a merger than in the day-to-day management of the organization that had been built by the senior generation, and the loneliness she felt as the sole voice of progress only worsened her situation. I know how difficult it is to nudge people who are set in their ways toward a shining tomorrow. Together, Fiona and I developed a strategy—relying on constructive dialogue with the senior generation and on well-developed leadership from Fiona's Gen Peer group—that would both help Fiona achieve her goals and keep her feeling fulfilled in the interim.

Not every successor needs a full-blown action plan and mediation strategy. Sometimes just one or two conversations can be enough to inspire the necessary change. I met with Miko only twice. He wanted his multi-branch family to function like the families featured in *Family Wealth: Keeping It in the Family*,[16] and to that end, he wanted to create a road map. Ten months later, he called with an update—he needed a few adjustments in the plan, but otherwise he was working solidly on his own.

The personal drive to solve your own problems is not unusual, and I am often in awe of those clients who see a problem and run straight at it. I had one client, Phil, who had suddenly and tumultuously left the family business—but four years later, he felt that his departure was still negatively affecting both him and the family. "Unfinished business," he called it. After meeting with him and his father and uncle (who still ran the business), Phil realized that resolving that conflict was up to him, and he committed himself to seeing a coach.

The conversations with Phil also allowed the senior generation to understand their past mistakes. They committed themselves to clarifying the rules of employment and to ensuring that their family

---

16 James Hughes Jr., *Family Wealth: Keeping It in the Family* (Princeton, NJ: Bloomberg Press, 2004).

would never again be rocked by the problem that had put Phil out in the cold. The work each side committed to was extensive, but my contribution was short and quick. I set things in motion, freed each side of the illusions that were holding them back, and empowered them to take action. They didn't need anything else from me.

But quick interventions don't always go so happily. Saul came to me to learn how to engage his father and uncle in a succession planning process, but as he described the situation, it became clear to me that the two senior partners would never agree to participate. Saul was wasting his best years working for founders who never intended to have successors. Once the facts had been laid out and Saul had had time to consider them, he realized that I'd picked up on a pattern that he was too close to see. It wasn't a happy conversation, but at the end of it, he had new clarity, which allowed him to build his own future outside of the family business.

* * *

Successors are people who, because of their ancestors' hard work, have a platform they can use to launch their own lives. Their personal growth, their careers, their social obligations, their family relationships, all may spring from this platform. True, the platform often comes with complexities. The opportunities it provides can be hidden by expectations, history, attitudes, and prejudices. But behind all that noise, the opportunities remain. Look for them. Learn from others who have walked a similar road, ask for help, and take advantage of the benefits you eventually find.

This book tells the stories of many different families who have found those benefits, who have taken on the challenging process of refining the good in their lives. The processes I've described can be difficult. They can take a long time, and the way forward isn't always painless. But it does work, if you're willing to commit to real change.

However, before you commit to any of it, ask yourself this question: **What's in it for me?** Every family journey is begun by one person who has their own, deeply personal reason for wanting things to be different. It's that one person who gets the ball rolling.

Beyond the "obvious" good of what you want to achieve, there must also be a personal motive: your personal growth, your personal peace of mind, your personal questions that are calling for answers. These are the motivations that will carry you forward in tough times, when other family members do not share your vision, and there is resistance all around. Everything else is the result of that first push. That's why the question, **What's in it for me?** is absolutely crucial to this process.

When you find your answer, when you know why you're choosing to change, you are ready to take those first steps on the path. It may be a long road, but your destination lies along it. I trust that you can get there.

And finally, the proverb at the beginning of this chapter highlights an important part of every successor's road to fulfillment. The language we use to describe ourselves and the world around us is essential to our own sense of possibility. I believe that mentally consigning ourselves to victimhood and powerlessness makes those states of mind real. Words have power. If you call yourself a victim, that's what you are.

But if you take the opposite tack, if you call out the things that make you strong, you can pull yourself out of any predicament. If you are willing to acknowledge the situation as it is and to talk about it with others, you may begin the change. As the proverb says, "those who love it will eat its produce."

Printed by Libri Plureos GmbH in Hamburg, Germany